THE
RETAIL
REVOLUTION

Transforming
Shopping
with Data

e k a
PUBLISHING

DHEERAJ AKULA

First Published in India by Eka Publishers 2024
Copyright © Eka Publishers

Printed and bound in India by Eka Publishers

ISBN: 979-83-04623-31-5

Title: The Retail Revolution: Transforming Shopping with Data
Author: Dheeraj Akula
Editor: Shruti Tyagi
Cover Design: Aniruddh Vaidya

1st Print December 2024

EKA PUBLISHERS
#118 Ushodaya Enclave, PO Miyapur
Hyderabad 500049. INDIA
ekapresshyderabad@gmail.com
+91 8008-101-590
www.ekapress.org

PREFACE

Welcome to "Retail Revolution - Transforming Shopping with Data," a comprehensive exploration of how machine learning and data-driven strategies reshape the retail landscape. This book is designed for retail professionals, business strategists, and enthusiasts looking to understand the transformative power of artificial intelligence in the retail sector. It aims to bridge the gap between technical concepts and practical, actionable applications by providing insights, case studies, and guidance on implementing machine learning in various aspects of retail management.

The motivation for writing this book stems from a clear trend in the retail industry toward increasing digitalization and automation. As consumer behaviors shift and technological advancements continue to accelerate, traditional retail models are being challenged. Machine learning offers unprecedented opportunities to enhance customer experiences, optimize operations, and secure and sustain competitive advantages. Yet, despite its potential, the practical application of machine learning in retail can seem daunting to those who have a technical background.

This book demystifies the process, breaking down complex algorithms into understandable segments and showing how they can be applied to real-world retail challenges. From personalizing customer interactions to streamlining supply chain logistics, each unit highlights specific areas where machine learning can significantly impact.

The structure of the book is designed to facilitate a gradual build-up of knowledge:
•Unit 1 dives into enhancing the customer experience through personalized marketing, recommendation systems, and behavior analysis. It explores how AI can transform every touchpoint of the customer journey.

•Unit 2 focuses on operational efficiency, covering inventory management, pricing strategies, and store layout optimization. These chapters are crucial for understanding how AI can reduce costs and improve margins in a competitive retail environment. Throughout the book, you'll find examples and case studies from leading retailers successfully integrating AI into their operations. These stories are intended to inspire and provide a clear sense of how theoretical concepts are translated into practice.

As we explore these topics, our goal is not just to inform but also to inspire action. Whether you are a retailer, a manager, or a business student, this book will provide you with the knowledge and tools to participate in the AI transformation of retail. We invite you to join us as we navigate the exciting and ever-evolving landscape of retail technology.

GITHUB LOCATION FOR THE DATA:
All the dataset mentioned in this book can be downloaded from: https://github.com/dheeraj-akula/RetailRevolution

ABOUT THE AUTHOR

Dheeraj Akula has had a career focused on B2C and B2B Services Sector with a major focus on transformation projects in Retail sector in India, USA, UK, etc. while working at Tata Consultancy Services, Tech Mahindra, Blue Yonder and Oracle. Through his work he has experienced technology enabling and transforming various functions in Retail. He went out further and made unique technology  innovations that lead to 3 US Patents being granted on IoT and Artificial Intelligence.

Dheeraj Akula has an MBA Degree and a PG Diploma from The Chartered Institute of Marketing in The United Kingdom. He has been living and working across the globe in Asia, Americas, Europe and Africa. He is currently based in the USA and travels across the globe to present at events.

This book is an attempt to get the insights from all those experiences into a structured text.

ABOUT THE EDITOR

 *Shruti is a passionate advocate for data-driven decision-making and a seasoned technology leader with over 15 years of experience. She specializes in data science, machine learning, generative AI, and SaaS. Shruti excels at transforming complex datasets into actionable insights and employs critical thinking to empower teams to leverage advanced analytics and visualization techniques for business growth. Outside of her professional pursuits, she is a devoted mother of two young children.*

A NOTE TO THE READERS

Dear Readers,

Thank you for choosing to embark on this journey through "Retail Revolution - Transforming Shopping with Data." As you turn these pages, you are set to explore the vibrant intersection of retail and technology, where data and machine learning are not just tools, but catalysts for transformation.

This book is born out of a passion for the potential of artificial intelligence to reshape the world of retail. This sector touches virtually every aspect of our daily lives. The rapidly evolving landscape of retail, driven by technological advances and changing consumer expectations, presents a thrilling arena for innovation. In writing this book, I have aimed to illuminate the path for retail professionals, students, and tech enthusiasts to leverage AI in impactful and sustainable ways.

The insights and strategies you will discover here are a culmination of extensive research, discussions with industry experts, and my personal observations of the trends shaping the future of retail. Each chapter is crafted with the intent to provide both depth and clarity, ensuring that whether you are a novice or a seasoned professional, you will find valuable knowledge to enhance your understanding and skills.

As you delve into the content, I encourage you to not only absorb the information but also challenge it. AI is dynamic, and true learning comes from questioning, experimenting, and adapting. I hope this book serves as a starting point for your own experiments with AI in retail, sparking ideas that you will develop further in your professional pursuits.

Lastly, I am genuinely eager to hear from you. Your feedback, questions, and stories of how you have applied these concepts will enrich this ongoing conversation. Please feel free to reach out through the channels provided, join our online community, or attend one of the many talks and workshops I conduct throughout the year.

Together, let's navigate the complexities of AI and data-driven technology to create smarter, more responsive retail experiences. Here's to building a future where technology enhances every facet of the shopping journey, making it more personalized, efficient, and enjoyable.

Warm regards,
DHEERAJ AKULA - *Author, Retail Revolution - Transforming Shopping with Data*

TABLE OF CONTENT

UNIT

1

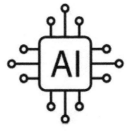

ENHANCING CUSTOMER EXPERIENCE WITH AI

CHAPTER 1

PERSONALIZED MARKETING

In the information age, the one-size-fits-all marketing approach is becoming increasingly ineffective. Today's consumers expect more - more relevance, more personalization, and more value. This chapter delves into how machine learning (ML) is revolutionizing the approach to marketing within the retail sector by enabling highly personalized, targeted campaigns that resonate with individual consumers.

The rapid evolution of digital technology has profoundly impacted marketing, with machine learning (ML) emerging as a pivotal force in reshaping marketing strategies across industries. By harnessing the power of ML, marketers are now equipped to analyze vast datasets, predict consumer behavior with remarkable accuracy, and deliver highly personalized customer experiences. This long note delves into the transformative role of machine learning in marketing, exploring its capabilities, applications, and the potential it holds for the future.

The Role of Machine Learning in Marketing

Machine learning is a subset of artificial intelligence that involves algorithms learning from data, identifying patterns, and making decisions with minimal human intervention. In marketing, ML is primarily used to process and analyze large amounts of data quickly and efficiently, allowing marketers to gain deeper insights into customer preferences, behaviors, and trends.

Key Capabilities of Machine Learning in Marketing

Predictive Analytics: ML excels in predictive analytics, which uses historical data to predict future outcomes. This translates to forecasting consumer behaviors, such as purchase patterns, product preferences, and potential churn rates in marketing. Businesses can craft proactive strategies that cater to future needs by predicting what customers might do next.

Customer Segmentation: Traditional customer segmentation often involves manual categorization based on demographic data. ML algorithms enhance this process by dynamically segmenting customers based on many behavioral data points, such as browsing history, purchase records, and social media activity. This dynamic segmentation helps deliver more tailored marketing messages that resonate with individual consumer needs.

Personalization: One of the most powerful applications of ML in marketing is the ability to personalize at scale. From personalized product recommendations to customized email marketing campaigns, ML analyzes individual consumer behaviors to deliver relevant and personalized content and offers. This enhances the consumer experience and significantly boosts conversion rates and customer loyalty.

Optimizing Marketing Campaigns: ML algorithms can optimize marketing campaigns in real time by continuously analyzing the effectiveness of different advertising channels and marketing messages. This involves A/B testing at scale, determining the best-performing strategies, and reallocating resources to maximize ROI.

Sentiment Analysis: By using natural language processing, a branch of ML, marketers can analyze customer sentiments across social media platforms, reviews, and customer feedback. Understanding public sentiment allows companies to proactively adjust their marketing strategies, address customer concerns, and improve their products and services.

Machine Learning for Customer Segmentation

Customer segmentation involves dividing a customer base into groups of similar individuals in specific ways relevant to marketing, such as age, gender, interests, and spending habits. ML algorithms enhance this process by identifying more nuanced segments based on complex patterns that would be difficult for humans to detect. For example, clustering algorithms can group customers based on their transaction history, website navigation patterns, and engagement with previous marketing campaigns.

Key Techniques:
- **Clustering:** Use K-means or hierarchical clustering algorithms to discover distinct customer groups.
- **Classification:** Employ techniques like decision trees or support vector machines to categorize customers based on predefined labels.

EXAMPLE: Let's take an example and dive deep into the implementation

Problem statement: How can we optimize our marketing strategy to increase customer engagement and retention?

Solution: This project analyzes customer behavior data to create targeted and personalized marketing strategies. We seek to understand customer segments and preferences by applying statistical techniques and providing actionable insights for improved engagement and retention.

Step 1: Importing Libraries and visualizing the data

```python
import numpy as np
import pandas as pd
from datetime import date
import seaborn as sns
import matplotlib.pyplot as plt
import warnings
warnings.filterwarnings('ignore')

data=pd.read_csv('D:\\datasets\\akularetailrevolution\\ma
rketing_campaign.csv',sep=';')
#checking the rows and columns
print("Shape: ",data.shape)

#check top 3 rows
print(data.head(3))

# Loop through each column and create a plot
for column in data.columns:
    # Check data type of the column
    if pd.api.types.is_numeric_dtype(data[column]):
        # Create a histogram for numeric data
        plt.figure(figsize=(10, 6))
        sns.histplot(data[column], kde=True)
        plt.title(f'Histogram of {column}')
        plt.xlabel(column)
        plt.ylabel('Frequency')
        plt.grid(True)
        plt.show()
    else:
        # Create a count plot for categorical data
```

```
        plt.figure(figsize=(10, 6))
        sns.countplot(x=column, data=data)
        plt.title(f'Count Plot of {column}')
        plt.xlabel(column)
        plt.ylabel('Count')
        plt.xticks(rotation=45)
        plt.grid(True)
        plt.show()
```

Step 2: Data preprocessing

```
#Creating new columns 'Age' and 'Spending'
data['Age']=2014-data['Year_Birth']
data['Spending']=data['MntWines']+data['MntFruits']+data[
'MntMeatProducts']+data['MntFishProducts']+data['MntSweet
Products']+data['MntGoldProds']

#Storing the latest data.
last_date=date(2014,6,29)
#Converting the Object datatype to datetime64 and storing
in the column "Seniority".
data['Seniority']=pd.to_datetime(data['Dt_Customer'],
dayfirst=True,format = '%Y-%m-%d')
#How many month old the customer is from the latest date
with the company is stored in "Seniority Column".
data['Seniority'] =
pd.to_numeric(data['Seniority'].dt.date.apply(lambda x:
(last_date - x)).dt.days, downcast='integer')/30

#Renaming the columns with appropriate names
data=data.rename(columns={'NumWebPurchases':"Web","NumCat
alogPurchases":"Catalog","NumStorePurchases":"Store"})

#print unique marital status values
print(data['Marital_Status'].unique())

#Categorizing the marital status into 'Alone' and 'In
couple'
data['Marital_Status']=data['Marital_Status'].replace({'D
ivorced':'Alone','Single':'Alone','Married':'In
couple','Together':'In
couple','Absurd':'Alone','Widow':'Alone','YOLO':'Alone'})
print(data['Marital_Status'].unique())
```

```python
# printing unique education values
print(data['Education'].unique())
#Converting education into 'undergraduate' and
 'postgraduate'
data['Education']=data['Education'].replace({'Graduation'
:'Postgraduate','PhD':'Postgraduate','Master':'Postgradua
te','Basic':'Undergraduate','2n Cycle':'Undergraduate'})
print(data['Education'].unique())

#adding total children column
data['Children']=data['Kidhome']+data['Teenhome']
#'Has_child' column to have 2 option 'Has child' and 'No
child'
data['Has_child']=np.where(data.Children>0,'Has
child','No child')

#change the column values of children
data['Children'].replace({3:"3 children",2:"2
children",1:"1 child",0:"No child"},inplace=True)

#Renaming more columns with relevant names
data=data.rename(columns={'MntWines':'Wines','MntFruits':
'Fruits','MntMeatProducts':'Meat','MntFishProducts':'Fish
','MntSweetProducts':'Sweets','MntGoldProds':'Gold'})

data=data[['Age','Education','Marital_Status','Income','S
pending','Seniority','Has_child','Children','Wines','Frui
ts','Meat','Fish','Sweets','Gold']]

#updated columns
print(data.head())

#Checking null values
print(data.isnull().sum())

#Dropped rows with Income as NaN
data=data.dropna(subset=['Income'])
print(data.isnull().sum())

# streamlining income details - removing outliers
print(data['Income'].describe())
```

```
#Calculate IQR=Q3-Q1
print("Inter Quartile Range (IQR) = ",68522-35303)

'''
Calculating upper bound outlier
Q3+1.5 x IQR, this is the upper bound for identifying
potential outliers. Any data point above this threshold
is considered a potential outlier. It is used in the
construction of box plots and is part of the Tukey's
fences method for outlier detection.
'''
print("Upper Bound Outlier: ",68522+(1.5*33219))

'''
Calculating lower bound outlier
Q3 -1.5 x IQR, this is the lower bound for identifying
potential outliers. Any data point below this threshold
is considered a potential outlier.
'''
#Q1-1.5 x IQR
print("Lower Bound Outlier: ",35303-(1.5*33219))

print("1. Data Shape: ",data.shape)
#There are 8 records which falls beyond upper bound
outlier, hence delete them.
data.drop(data[data['Income']>=118350.5].index,inplace=Tr
ue)
print("2. Data Shape: ",data.shape)
```

STEP 3: Clustering the data distribution

We will create 4 categories:

1. Old customers with high income and high spending nature.
2. New customers with below-average income and low-spending nature
3. New customers with high income and high spending nature
4. Old customers with below-average income and low-spending nature

```
from sklearn.preprocessing import StandardScaler,
normalize

# Step 3: Making clusters
'''
```

```
Standardizing or scaling numerical features in a dataset
After this process, scaled_data will contain the
standardized versions of the 'Income', 'Seniority', and
'Spending' columns from the original dataset.
Standardization is a common preprocessing step in machine
learning to ensure that different features are on a
similar scale, preventing certain features from
dominating others during model training.
'''
scaler=StandardScaler()
dataset_temp=data[['Income','Seniority','Spending']]
scaled_data=pd.DataFrame(scaler.fit_transform(dataset_tem
p))

print(scaled_data.head())

'''
Normalizing the data using L2 Norm
Applying L2 normalization to each row of scaled_data,
ensuring that the squared sum of values in each row is
equal to 1. The result is stored in the variable X.

Normalization is often used to standardize the scale of
features, and L2 normalization specifically ensures that
each data point is represented as a unit vector in
Euclidean space.
'''

X=normalize(scaled_data,norm='l2')
```

STEP 4: Creating Gaussian Model

A Gaussian Mixture Model (GMM) is a probabilistic model commonly used for clustering and density estimation in machine learning and statistics. GMM is a generative probabilistic model that represents a mixture of multiple Gaussian distributions. Each Gaussian distribution (component) in the mixture represents a cluster within the dataset. GMM is particularly useful when dealing with datasets that exhibit complex structures and when the underlying data distribution is assumed to be a combination of multiple Gaussian distributions.

Here are the key concepts and components of a Gaussian Mixture Model:

The mixture of Gaussians:

GMM assumes that a mixture of several Gaussian distributions generates the dataset. Each Gaussian component represents a cluster within the data.

Parameters:
The key parameters of a GMM include the mean, covariance, and weight for each Gaussian component. The mean and covariance determine the shape and orientation of each Gaussian distribution, while the weight represents the contribution of each component to the overall mixture.

Probability Density Function (PDF):
The probability density function of a GMM is a weighted sum of the individual Gaussian distributions. Mathematically, it is expressed as the sum of the products of the weights and the Gaussian PDFs of each component.

Expectation-Maximization (EM) Algorithm:
The parameters of a GMM are typically estimated using the Expectation-Maximization (EM) algorithm. The EM algorithm iteratively refines the estimates of the mean, covariance, and weight parameters based on the observed data.

Cluster Assignment:
GMM assigns a probability of belonging to each cluster for each data point rather than a hard assignment. This probabilistic nature allows GMM to handle overlapping clusters more effectively.

Covariance Type:
GMM supports different types of covariance structures, such as spherical, diagonal, tied, or full covariance. The choice of covariance type influences the shape and orientation of the Gaussian distributions.

Number of Components:
The number of Gaussian components (clusters) is a hyperparameter that needs to be specified before fitting the model. The optimal number of components is often determined using techniques like the Akaike Information Criterion (AIC) or the Bayesian Information Criterion (BIC).

Applications of Gaussian Mixture Models include:
- Clustering: Identifying natural groupings or clusters within a dataset.
- Density Estimation: Modeling the underlying probability distribution of the data.
- Anomaly Detection: Detecting unusual patterns or outliers in the data.

```python
from sklearn.mixture import GaussianMixture
import plotly.graph_objects as go

# Step 4: Creating Gaussian Model
gmm=GaussianMixture(n_components=4,covariance_type='spher
ical',max_iter=2000,random_state=5).fit(X)
labels=gmm.predict(X)
dataset_temp['Cluster']=labels
dataset_temp=dataset_temp.replace({0:'Stars',1:'Need
attention',2:'High potential',3:'Leaky bucket'})

print(labels)

# Merge data and dataset_temp.Cluster
data=data.merge(dataset_temp.Cluster,left_index=True,righ
t_index=True)

print(data.columns)

#  Floating-point numbers rounded to zero decimal places
due to the applied float formatting option.
pd.options.display.float_format="{:.0f}".format

summary=data[['Income','Spending','Seniority','Cluster']]
summary.set_index('Cluster',inplace=True)
summary=summary.groupby('Cluster').describe().transpose()
print("\n\nSummary \n----------\n",summary)

#Plot this data to see the customer clustering
PLOT=go.Figure()
for C in list(data.Cluster.unique()):

PLOT.add_trace(go.Scatter3d(x=data[data.Cluster==C]['Inco
me'],

y=data[data.Cluster==C]['Seniority'],

z=data[data.Cluster==C]['Spending'],
mode='markers',marker_size=6,marker_line_width=1,
name=str(C)))
PLOT.update_traces(hovertemplate='Income: %{x}
<br>Seniority: %{y} <br>Spending: %{z}')
```

```
PLOT.update_layout(width=800,height=800,autosize=True,sho
wlegend=True,
scene=dict(xaxis=dict(title='Income',titlefont_color='bla
ck'),
yaxis=dict(title='Seniority',titlefont_color='black'),
zaxis=dict(title='Spending',titlefont_color='black')),
font=dict(family="Gilroy",color='black',size=12))
PLOT.show()
```

Step 5: Data Preparation for Customer Personality Analysis

```
# Step 5: Data Preparation for Customer Personality
Analysis
#Creating Age Segment
cut_labels_Age=['Young','Adult','Mature','Senior']
cut_bins=[0,30,45,65,120]
data['Age_group']=pd.cut(data['Age'],bins=cut_bins,labels
=cut_labels_Age)
```

```python
print("1. Data: \n",data.head())
#Creating Income Segment
cut_labels_Income=['Low income','Low to medium
income','Medium to high income','High income']
data['Income_group']=pd.qcut(data['Income'],q=4,labels=cu
t_labels_Income)

print("2. Data: \n",data.head())

#Creating seniority segment
cut_labels_Seniority=['New customers','Discovering
customers','Experienced customers','Old customers']
data['Seniority_group']=pd.qcut(data['Seniority'],q=4,lab
els=cut_labels_Seniority)
data=data.drop(columns=['Age','Income','Seniority'])

print("3. Data: \n",data.head())

'''
Creating More segmentation based on spending habbit
'''
cut_labels=['Low consumer','Frequent consumer','Biggest
consumer']
data['Wines_segment']=pd.qcut(data['Wines'][data['Wines']
>0],q=[0,.25,.75,1],labels=cut_labels).astype("object")

data['Fruits_segment']=pd.qcut(data['Fruits'][data['Fruit
s']>0],q=[0,.25,.75,1],labels=cut_labels).astype("object"
)
data['Meat_segment']=pd.qcut(data['Meat'][data['Meat']>0]
,q=[0,.25,.75,1],labels=cut_labels).astype("object")
data['Fish_segment']=pd.qcut(data['Fish'][data['Fish']>0]
,q=[0,.25,.75,1],labels=cut_labels).astype("object")
data['Sweets_segment']=pd.qcut(data['Sweets'][data['Sweet
s']>0],q=[0,.25,.75,1],labels=cut_labels).astype("object"
)
data['Gold_segment']=pd.qcut(data['Gold'][data['Gold']>0]
,q=[0,.25,.75,1],labels=cut_labels).astype("object")
data.replace(np.nan,'Non consumer',inplace=True)
data.drop(columns=['Spending','Wines','Fruits','Meat','Fi
sh','Sweets','Gold'],inplace=True)
data=data.astype(object)
```

```
print("4. Data: \n",data.head())
```

Step 6: Association Rule

An association rule is a statement that expresses a relationship between items in a dataset based on their co-occurrence patterns. It is a fundamental concept in association rule mining, a data mining technique and machine learning technique.

Association rules are typically represented in the form of "if-then" statements, indicating that if a certain set of items (the antecedent) is present, then another set of items (the consequent) is likely to occur as well. The rules are derived from analyzing transactional data, where items are frequently bought or used together.

Here's a breakdown of the components of an association rule:

Antecedent: The "if" part of the rule. It represents a set of items observed or found together in the dataset.

Consequent: The "then" part of the rule. It represents another set of items that tends to occur along with the antecedent.

Support: The support of a rule is the proportion of transactions in the dataset that contain both the antecedent and the consequent. It indicates how frequently the rule is applicable.

Confidence: The confidence of a rule measures the reliability of the rule. It is the proportion of transactions containing the antecedent where the consequent is also present.

Lift: Lift is a measure that compares the observed support of the rule with the expected support if the antecedent and the consequent were independent. A lift value greater than 1 suggests a positive correlation between the items.

Here's an example of an association rule:

{Milk, Bread} => {Eggs}

This rule can be interpreted as: "If a customer buys Milk and Bread, then they are likely to buy Eggs as well."

APRIORI ALGORITHM

The Apriori algorithm is a popular algorithm used in data mining and machine learning to discover patterns in large datasets. It's particularly well-known for association rule mining, where the goal is to find relationships between different items in a dataset. Here's an overview of how the Apriori algorithm works:

Itemset:

The algorithm starts by identifying all the unique items present in the dataset. Each unique item is called an "itemset."

Support Count:

The algorithm then counts how often each item or combination of items appears in the dataset. This count is known as the "support count."

Setting Support Threshold:

A minimum support threshold is set. This threshold determines the minimum frequency an itemset must have to be considered interesting. Items or combinations below this threshold are discarded.

Generating Candidate Itemsets:

The algorithm generates new candidate itemsets by combining the remaining frequent itemsets. It creates larger combinations to explore more complex patterns.

Pruning:

These candidate itemsets are then pruned to eliminate those not meeting the minimum support threshold.

Repeat:

Steps 3 to 5 are repeated iteratively until no more frequent itemsets can be found.

Association Rule Generation:

Finally, association rules are generated from the frequent itemsets. These rules express relationships between different items, indicating that if one item or set of items is present, another item or set of items is likely to be present as well.

```
# Step 6: Association Rule

from sklearn import metrics
from mlxtend.frequent_patterns import apriori
from mlxtend.frequent_patterns import association_rules

# Displays all columns when showing pandas DataFrames.
pd.set_option('display.max_columns',None)
# Displays all rows when showing pandas DataFrames.
pd.set_option('display.max_rows',None)
# Sets the maximum column width to 999 characters,
allowing for complete visibility of long text or URLs.
pd.set_option('display.max_colwidth',999)
# Formats floating-point numbers to display three decimal
places.
pd.options.display.float_format="{:.3f}".format
# Creates a copy of the original dataset called
association.
association=data.copy()
# Converts categorical variables into dummy/indicator
variables using one-hot encoding.
df=pd.get_dummies(association)
# Specifies the minimum support threshold for itemsets in
the Apriori algorithm.
min_support=0.08
# Sets the maximum length of the itemsets to consider.
max_len=10
# Applies the Apriori algorithm to find frequent itemsets
in the dataset.
frequent_items=apriori(df,use_colnames=True,min_support=m
in_support,max_len=max_len+1)
# Generates association rules from the frequent itemsets
using the lift metric.
rules=association_rules(frequent_items,metric='lift',min_
threshold=1)
rules.head()
```

Let's take the 1st row above and break down the information
Antecedents and Consequents:

Antecedents: (Marital_Status_Alone) **Consequents:** (Education_Postgraduate)

Here, we want to see if there's any connection between Maritial_Status_Alone and postgraduate education.

Antecedent Support: 0.356 (35.6% of people are alone in terms of marital status) **Consequent Support:** 0.885 (88.5% of people have a postgraduate education)

This tells us how common each group is in the entire dataset.

Support: 0.317 (31.7% of people are both alone in terms of marital status and have a postgraduate education)

This shows how many people in the dataset fall into both categories.

Confidence: 0.893 (89.3% confidence)

This means that if someone is alone in terms of marital status, there's an 89.3% chance that they also have a postgraduate education.

Lift: 1.009 (Slightly above 1)

Lift tells us whether the relationship between the antecedent and consequent is stronger than what would be expected by chance. A lift of 1.009 indicates a slight positive correlation.

Leverage: 0.003

Leverage measures the difference between the observed frequency of the antecedent and consequent appearing together and the frequency that would be expected if they were independent.

Conviction: 1.075

Conviction is a measure of how much the consequent relies on the antecedent. A conviction of 1.075 indicates a slight dependency.

In simpler terms, this row tells us that there is a strong association between people who are alone in terms of marital status and having a postgraduate education. About 31.7% of people in the dataset fall into both categories, and if someone is alone in terms of marital status, there's an 89.3% chance they also have a postgraduate education. The relationship is slightly stronger than expected by chance.

STEP 7: DRAWING INSIGHTS

```
# Step 7: Drawing Insights

product='Wines'
segment='Biggest consumer'
target='{\'%s_segment_%s\'}' %(product,segment)
results_personal_care=rules[rules['consequents'].astype(s
tr).str.contains(target,na=False)].sort_values(by='confid
ence',ascending=False)
print("Results:\n",results_personal_care.head())
```

Sample Output:

	consequents	antecedent support	consequent support	support	confidence	lift
9502	(Wines_segment_Biggest consumer)	0.113	0.248	0.081	0.719	2.896
4841	(Wines_segment_Biggest consumer)	0.123	0.248	0.086	0.701	2.825
4854	(Wines_segment_Biggest consumer)	0.124	0.248	0.085	0.689	2.775
9530	(Wines_segment_Biggest consumer)	0.123	0.248	0.082	0.662	2.666
4835	(Wines_segment_Biggest consumer)	0.121	0.248	0.080	0.660	2.661

INSIGHTS

Biggest Customers of Wines are

- Customer with an average income of 50000 or more.
- Customer with an average total spend 1200 or more.
- Customers registered with the company for 21 months approx.
- Customers with graduate degrees.
- also Customers who are heavy consumers of meat products.

Machine Learning for Personalized Promotions

Personalized Promotions

Once segments are identified, machine learning helps tailor marketing messages that cater to the unique preferences of each segment. For instance, predictive analytics can forecast which products new mothers will most likely purchase, allowing retailers to offer targeted discounts on baby products to this segment.

Key Strategies:
- **Predictive Targeting:** Regression analysis is used to predict customer responses to promotional activities.
- **Recommendation Systems:** Implement systems that use customers' past behavior to suggest relevant products.

Let's take a scenario: A Large Apparel Retail Chain

Imagine a large apparel retail chain looking to enhance its marketing efforts by introducing personalized promotions tailored to individual customers' preferences and purchase histories. This strategy aims to increase customer satisfaction, encourage repeat business, and maximize sales.

Step 1: Data Collection

The first step involves collecting and integrating data from various sources:
- **Transactional Data:** Includes details from past purchases, such as item types, quantities bought, and transaction amounts.
- **Customer Demographics:** Age, gender, geographic location, and possibly income levels.
- **Online Interaction Data:** Data gathered from the retailer's website and mobile app, including page views, clicks, wish lists, and cart history.
- **Social Media Engagement:** Insights from social media platforms indicate customer preferences and lifestyle choices.

Sample data would look something like this, here's a breakdown of the columns you might include:

1. **CustomerID**: A unique identifier for each customer.
2. **Age**: Customer's age.
3. **Gender**: Customer's gender (Male, Female, Other).
4. **Location**: Geographical location of the customer.
5. **AnnualIncome**: Approximate annual income of the customer.
6. **TotalTransactions**: Total number of transactions made by the customer in the past year.
7. **TotalAmountSpent**: Total amount spent in the past year.
8. **AverageTransactionValue**: Average spending per transaction.
9. **NumberOfStoreVisits**: Number of times customer visited the store.
10. **NumberOfOnlineVisits**: Number of times customer visited the website.
11. **FavoriteCategory**: The category from which most products were purchased (e.g., Apparel, Electronics, Home Goods).
12. **LastPurchaseDate**: Date of the last purchase.

13. **PromotionResponded**: Whether the customer responded to the last promotion (1 for yes, 0 for no).

Snapshot of the data:

CustomerID	Age	Gender	Location	AnnualIncome	TotalTransactions	TotalAmountSpent	AverageTransactionValue	NumberOfStoreVisits	NumberOfOnlineVisits	FavoriteCategory	LastPurchaseDate	PromotionResponded
1	56	Other	Urban	60254	35	910	26	3	32	Home Goods	2021-01-01 00:00:00	0
2	69	Other	Suburban	87418	12	468	39	28	12	Electronics	2021-01-02 00:00:00	0
3	46	Other	Suburban	44472	26	1248	48	12	40	Electronics	2021-01-03 00:00:00	0
4	32	Male	Rural	33471	19	475	25	3	41	Electronics	2021-01-04 00:00:00	0
5	60	Other	Suburban	38329	45	1620	36	4	46	Electronics	2021-01-05 00:00:00	1
6	25	Male	Suburban	64865	7	126	18	25	36	Home Goods	2021-01-06 00:00:00	1
7	38	Female	Rural	76850	47	2115	45	21	15	Apparel	2021-01-07 00:00:00	1
8	56	Other	Suburban	84220	7	287	41	3	44	Electronics	2021-01-08 00:00:00	1

Figure 1: Snapshot of the data - sample

Step 2: Data Preparation

Data needs to be cleaned and organized to be usable:

- **Cleaning Data:** Handling missing values, removing duplicates, and correcting errors.
- **Feature Engineering:** Creating new variables from existing data that can help in the prediction process, such as calculating the average spend per visit, purchase frequency, and preferred shopping channels.

Step 3: Building the Machine Learning Model

With data ready, the next step is building the model that will predict which promotions or products a customer is likely to be interested in:

- **Choosing a Model:** Decision trees, random forests, or gradient boosting machines are good starting points due to their ability to handle different types of data and their interpretability.
- **Training the Model:** Use historical data to train the model. The target variable could be whether a customer redeemed a specific type of offer in the past.
- **Validation:** Using a separate validation set to evaluate the model's performance to avoid overfitting and ensure that it generalizes well to new data.

Step 4: Implementation of Personalized Promotions

Using the insights and predictions from the model:

- **Targeted Offers:** Customers predicted to be interested in certain product categories might receive discounts on those categories. For instance, a customer who frequently buys children's clothing might get a promotion for back-to-school items.

- **Dynamic Email Marketing:** Send personalized email campaigns featuring products that individual customers are most likely to buy, based on their model-predicted preferences.
- **App Notifications:** For app users, push notifications about promotions on products they have shown interest in or added to their wish list can drive immediate engagement.

Step 5: Monitoring and Optimization

After implementing personalized promotions:

- **A/B Testing:** Systematically test different versions of promotional content among similar customer groups to see which performs better and refine the approach based on results.
- **Feedback Loop:** Use customer responses to promotions, both positive and negative, to further train and refine the machine learning models. This feedback loop helps in adapting to changing customer preferences over time.

DESIGN SOLUTION

To design a complete implementation for a machine learning model that predicts customer responses to personalized promotions based on the synthetic dataset generated, we'll go through the following steps:

1. Data Preprocessing
2. Model Training
3. Model Evaluation
4. Generating Insights

```python
# Step 1: Data Preprocessing
import pandas as pd
import numpy as np
from sklearn.model_selection import train_test_split
from sklearn.preprocessing import LabelEncoder
from sklearn.ensemble import RandomForestClassifier
from sklearn.metrics import accuracy_score,
classification_report
import matplotlib.pyplot as plt

# Generate the dataset
np.random.seed(42)
n_samples = 1000
data =
```

```
pd.read_csv("D:\\datasets\\akularetailrevolution\\retail_
data_sample.csv")

# Encode categorical data
label_encoders = {}
for column in ['Gender', 'Location', 'FavoriteCategory']:
    le = LabelEncoder()
    data[column] = le.fit_transform(data[column])
    label_encoders[column] = le

# Split data into features and target
X = data.drop(['CustomerID', 'LastPurchaseDate',
'PromotionResponded'], axis=1)
y = data['PromotionResponded']

# Split data into training and testing sets
X_train, X_test, y_train, y_test = train_test_split(X, y,
test_size=0.2, random_state=42)


'''
Step 2: Model Training
We'll use a RandomForestClassifier due to its robustness
and ability to handle imbalanced data.
'''
# Train the model
model = RandomForestClassifier(n_estimators=100,
random_state=42)
model.fit(X_train, y_train)


'''
Step 3: Model Evaluation
We'll evaluate the model using accuracy and a
classification report.
'''
# Predict on the test set
y_pred = model.predict(X_test)

# Calculate accuracy
accuracy = accuracy_score(y_test, y_pred)
print(f'Accuracy: {accuracy:.2f}')

# Classification report
print(classification_report(y_test, y_pred))
```

```
'''
Step 4: Generating Insights
We'll visualize feature importances to understand what
drives promotional responses.
'''
# Plot feature importances
feature_importances =
pd.Series(model.feature_importances_, index=X.columns)
feature_importances.nlargest(10).plot(kind='barh')
plt.title('Feature Importances')
plt.show()
```

The implementation of a machine learning model for predicting customer responses to personalized promotions provides retailers with a multitude of valuable insights. By analyzing the behavior of customers in response to past promotions and various customer-specific features, retailers can refine their marketing strategies, enhance customer engagement, and ultimately boost sales efficiency. Here are detailed insights that retailers can gather from this process:

1. Understanding Customer Preferences
The analysis can reveal which types of promotions are most effective with different segments of the customer base. For instance, data might show that younger customers respond better to digital marketing campaigns on social media, whereas older customers may favor discount coupons used in physical stores. This allows retailers to customize their promotional efforts according to the preferences of different demographic groups.

2. Optimizing Promotion Timing
By analyzing when customers have historically responded to promotions (e.g., seasonality, weekdays vs. weekends, during specific events), retailers can time their campaigns to coincide with periods of higher engagement. This optimization ensures that promotions are not only targeted but also timely, increasing the likelihood of success.

3. Improving Resource Allocation
Understanding which promotions work and which do not allow retailers to allocate their marketing budgets more effectively. Resources can be channelled into

campaigns and strategies that yield the highest return on investment, thereby maximizing the efficiency of marketing expenditures.

4. Enhancing Personalization

The machine learning model helps identify the most relevant variables that influence whether a customer will respond to a promotion. These variables can include product preferences, shopping frequency, average transaction value, and more. With this knowledge, retailers can craft highly personalized offers that resonate well with individual customers or specific customer segments, thus increasing the conversion rate.

5. Predicting Customer Lifetime Value

By combining insights from promotional responses with overall purchase patterns, retailers can better predict customer lifetime value (CLV). This metric is crucial for making informed decisions about how much to invest in retaining existing customers and acquiring new ones.

6. Reducing Campaign Fatigue

Overexposure to promotions can lead to campaign fatigue, where customers become desensitized to marketing efforts. Insights from the model can help retailers avoid this by identifying the optimal frequency of promotions for different customer segments, ensuring that marketing efforts remain fresh and effective.

7. Detecting and Reducing Churn

The model can also help identify early signs of customer churn. Customers who have stopped responding to promotions may be at risk of churning. Retailers can then target these individuals with special retention campaigns designed to re-engage them before they leave.

8. Feature Importance Analysis

The machine learning process typically involves an analysis of feature importance, which helps retailers understand which factors most significantly impact the success of their promotional campaigns. For instance, if the feature 'Annual Income' is highly predictive, promotions might be adjusted according to income levels. Similarly, if 'Location' plays a crucial role, local tastes and preferences need more consideration in campaign designs.

9. Adapting to Trends

As consumer behavior evolves, the continuous learning aspect of machine learning models ensures that the retailer's strategies evolve as well. By regularly updating the model with new data, retailers can stay ahead of trends and continuously refine their approach.

Case Studies

Applications and Real-World Examples

Several leading companies have successfully leveraged ML to revolutionize their marketing efforts:

Amazon: Amazon's recommendation engine is one of the best examples of ML in marketing. It analyzes past purchase behavior, items in the shopping cart, items rated and liked, and what other customers have viewed and purchased to recommend products dynamically.

Google: Google AdWords uses machine learning to optimize the effectiveness of ad campaigns. By analyzing user data, Google can deliver ads that are more likely to be clicked, ensuring higher effectiveness for advertisers and more relevant ads for users.

Spotify: Spotify uses ML to personalize playlists and recommend music tracks to users. By understanding individual listening habits and preferences, Spotify can tailor its music recommendations to keep users engaged.

CASE STUDY 1: STARBUCKS

Background: Starbucks uses its loyalty card and mobile app to collect data on purchase behavior, which is then analyzed to customize marketing messages and offers.

Implementation: Machine learning algorithms analyze customers' purchase history and preferences to offer personalized discounts and recommendations directly through the app.

Outcome: This approach increased user engagement and boosted sales significantly, demonstrating the power of personalized marketing to enhance customer satisfaction and loyalty.

CASE STUDY 2: SEPHORA

Background: Sephora leverages in-store and online interaction data to create a unified customer profile, which is used to personalize communications and recommendations.

Implementation: Using facial recognition software in stores and machine learning algorithms online, Sephora offers personalized makeup tutorials and product recommendations.

Outcome: These personalized experiences have improved customer satisfaction and increased sales across multiple channels.

CASE STUDY 3: NETFLIX

Background: Although not a traditional retailer, Netflix's use of personalized marketing in the entertainment sector offers valuable insights. Netflix uses machine learning to tailor its viewing recommendations based on user behavior.

Implementation: By analyzing data collected from millions of users about viewing times, pauses, and preferences, Netflix's algorithms predict which new shows users will enjoy watching.

Outcome: Netflix reports that these personalized recommendations significantly influence viewing choices, keeping subscribers engaged and reducing churn rates.

Conclusion

While ML offers numerous benefits in marketing, it also presents challenges and ethical concerns. Data privacy is a significant issue, as using personal data in ML models can lead to privacy violations if not handled correctly. Marketers must navigate the fine line between personalization and privacy, ensuring compliance with data protection regulations such as GDPR.

Furthermore, there is the risk of bias in ML models, where algorithms may inherit and amplify existing biases in the data. Marketers must continuously monitor and update their models to avoid discriminatory practices and ensure fairness.

Personalized marketing, powered by machine learning, represents a paradigm shift in how retailers interact with consumers. By leveraging complex algorithms to analyze data and predict trends, retailers can create marketing strategies that are not only responsive but also anticipatory, offering consumers what they want, often before they know they want it.

This chapter has explored the foundational techniques of ML in marketing, illuminated by case studies from leading companies. As machine learning technology advances, the potential for even more sophisticated personalization grows, promising exciting opportunities for retailers willing to invest in these technologies.

Looking ahead, the role of ML in marketing is set to grow even more significantly. Advances in AI and machine learning, such as deep learning, open new possibilities for even more sophisticated analysis and automation. As technology evolves, so too will how businesses interact with their customers.

In conclusion, machine learning has transformed marketing from a guessing game into a precise science. As businesses continue to navigate the digital landscape, implementing ML will be key to staying competitive and delivering value to customers. Marketers must embrace these technologies, continually learn and adapt, and responsibly leverage the power of ML to forge deeper connections with consumers.

* * *

CHAPTER 2

PRODUCT RECOMMENDATION SYSTEMS

In today's competitive e-commerce landscape, personalized product recommendations are more than a luxury—they are an expectation. This chapter explores the sophisticated mechanisms behind product recommendation systems, the backbone of modern retail and e-commerce platforms. We will delve into the design of these engines and their integration into e-commerce platforms for real-time, dynamic product suggestions that enhance user experience and boost sales.

Understanding Product Recommendation Systems

Product recommendation systems are specialized algorithms designed to suggest relevant products to users based on various factors, including but not limited to their browsing history, purchase history, demographic data, and preferences. These systems leverage machine learning techniques to predict user preferences and recommend products accordingly.

How Product Recommendation Systems Work

Product recommendation systems typically use three main types of filtering methods to provide suggestions:

- **Collaborative Filtering:** This method makes recommendations based on the collective behavior of users. It assumes that if users A and B have similar preferences, then the recommendations for user A can be informed by the preferences of user B and vice versa. Collaborative filtering can be further divided into two sub-types:

  - **User-Based Collaborative Filtering:** This approach recommends products by finding similar users. This is often based on observing and matching user behaviors, such as purchases or ratings.

  - **Item-Based Collaborative Filtering:** This technique recommends items that are similar to items the user has liked before. It often uses item ratings to identify products that share similar rating patterns.

- **Content-Based Filtering:** Unlike collaborative filtering that relies on user interaction data, content-based filtering recommends items based on the features of the items themselves and a profile of the user's preferences. For example, if a user has shown a preference for thriller novels, the system might recommend books from the same genre.

- **Hybrid Approaches:** These systems combine collaborative filtering, content-based filtering, and sometimes other methods to improve recommendation performance and overcome certain limitations of standalone systems. For example, a hybrid approach might use content-based filtering to handle situations where user interaction data is sparse (cold start problem) and collaborative filtering to provide deeper personalization as more user data becomes available.

Data Sources for Recommendation Systems

- **Transactional Data:** Records of what customers have bought, such as time of purchase, quantity, and product details.

- **Behavioral Data:** Data on how customers interact with a website or app, including clicks, cart additions, page views, and time spent on pages.

- **Demographic Data:** Information about the customers themselves, like age, gender, geographic location, and income level.

- **Content Data:** Detailed information about the products, including descriptions, categories, price, and specifications.

Techniques and Technologies

- **Machine Learning Models:** Advanced models, including matrix factorization, clustering algorithms, and neural networks, are used to predict user preferences and match products.

- **Natural Language Processing (NLP):** Used in content-based systems to analyze and interpret the textual descriptions of items.

- **Deep Learning:** Techniques like Convolutional Neural Networks (CNNs) for image analysis and Recurrent Neural Networks (RNNs) for sequence prediction are increasingly being used to enhance recommendation accuracy.

Key Objectives of Recommendation Systems

1. **Increase Sales:** By suggesting relevant products, these systems can increase the probability of purchases.

2. **Improve Customer Experience:** Tailored suggestions make the shopping experience more personal and convenient, which enhances customer satisfaction and loyalty.
3. **Optimize Inventory Management:** Businesses can better manage inventory levels by promoting products based on sales forecasts and popularity.

Designing Recommendation Engines

The development of an effective recommendation engine involves several key steps and considerations:

Data Collection

Gathering data is the first crucial step in building a recommendation system. Relevant data includes:

- **User Data:** Demographics, session length, frequency of visits.
- **Product Data:** Categories, price, availability, specifications.
- **Interaction Data:** Clicks, purchases, ratings, reviews.

Choosing the Right Algorithm

Several algorithms can be used to build recommendation systems, each with its strengths and use cases:

- **Collaborative Filtering:** This method makes recommendations based on the collective preferences of other users. It is subdivided into:
    - *User-based Collaborative Filtering:* Recommends products by finding similar users.
    - *Item-based Collaborative Filtering:* Recommends products that are similar to ones the user has liked before.

- **Content-Based Filtering:** This technique uses features of the products themselves to make recommendations suitable for situations with detailed metadata about each product.

- **Hybrid Systems:** Combining collaborative and content-based methods to utilize the strengths of both.

Building the Model

Building a recommendation engine model involves:

- **Preprocessing Data:** Cleaning and transforming data into a usable format.
- **Training the Model:** Using historical data to train the algorithm.
- **Evaluation:** Testing the model on unseen data to assess its effectiveness.

INTEGRATING AI INTO E-COMMERCE PLATFORMS FOR REAL-TIME RECOMMENDATIONS

Infrastructure Requirements

- **Robust IT Infrastructure:** Sufficient server capabilities and fast processing speeds are essential for handling large volumes of data and delivering recommendations in real time.

- **Seamless Data Integration:** Effective mechanisms must be in place to continuously gather and update user and product data.

Implementation Strategies

- **Real-time Data Processing:** Utilizing streaming data platforms like Apache Kafka to process user interactions in real-time.

- **Dynamic Recommendation Models:** Updating models as new data comes in to reflect the latest user preferences and trends.

- **Personalized User Experiences:** Customizing the UI/UX to display personalized recommendations dynamically based on real-time user data.

Project: Product Recommendation System for e-commerce

A proficiently developed recommendation system can significantly enhance the shopping experience for users on a website, thereby leading to improved customer acquisition and retention. The recommendation system we will design here will track a new customer's journey from their first visit to the website to when they start making repeat purchases.

This recommendation system is structured into three parts to fit the business context:

1. **Part I: Popular Product-Based System for New Customers** - This component targets new visitors by recommending currently popular products.

2. **Part II: Model-Based Collaborative Filtering** - It utilizes the customer's purchase history and ratings from other users who have bought similar products to provide more personalized recommendations.

3. **Part III: Initial Setup Without Product Ratings** - This part focuses on scenarios where a business is launching its e-commerce platform for the first time and lacks product ratings.

When a new visitor with no prior purchase history arrives at the e-commerce site, they are shown the most popular products available. After the first purchase, the recommendation system updates its suggestions by incorporating other users' ratings and using collaborative filtering techniques to recommend products that align with the visitor's purchase history.

Recommendation System - Part I: Product popularity-based recommendation system targeted at new customers

Popularity is a great strategy to target new customers with the most popular products sold on a business's website, and it is very useful when starting a recommendation engine.

```python
# Importing libraries
import pandas as pd
import matplotlib.pyplot as plt

plt.style.use("ggplot")

#Loading the dataset
ratings =
pd.read_csv('D:\\datasets\\akularetailrevolution\\ratings
_Beauty.csv')
ratings = ratings.dropna()
ratings.head()

print("Data shape: ",ratings.shape)

popular_products =
pd.DataFrame(ratings.groupby('ProductId')['Rating'].count
())
most_popular = popular_products.sort_values('Rating',
ascending=False)
print("Popular Products: ",most_popular.head(10))

#plot bar graph
most_popular.head(30).plot(kind = "bar")
plt.show()
```

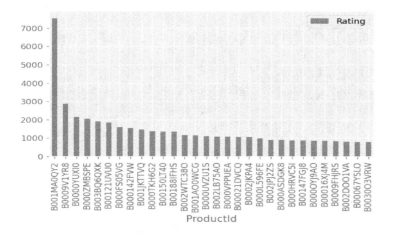

Insights:

The above graph gives us the most popular products (arranged in descending order) the business sells. For example, product ID # B001MA0QY2 has sales of over 7000, the next most popular product ID # B0009V1YR8, has sales of 3000, etc.

Recommendation System - Part II: Model-based collaborative filtering system

Recommend items to users based on purchase history and similar ratings provided by other users who bought items for a particular customer. A model-based collaborative filtering technique is chosen here as it helps predict products for a particular user by identifying patterns based on preferences from multiple user data.

Utility Matrix based on products sold and user reviews

Utility Matrix : A utility matrix consists of all possible user-item preferences (ratings) details represented as a matrix. The utility matrix is sparse, as no users would buy all the items in the list. Hence, most of the values are unknown.

```
# Importing libraries
import numpy as np
import pandas as pd
import matplotlib.pyplot as plt

plt.style.use("ggplot")

from sklearn.decomposition import TruncatedSVD

#Loading the dataset
```

```
ratings =
pd.read_csv('D:\\datasets\\akularetailrevolution\\ratings
_Beauty.csv')
ratings = ratings.dropna()
ratings.head()

print("Data shape: ",ratings.shape)

# Subset of Ratings
ratings1 = ratings.head(10000)
ratings_utility_matrix =
ratings1.pivot_table(values='Rating', index='UserId',
columns='ProductId', fill_value=0)
print("Utility Matrix:\n",ratings_utility_matrix.head())

#As expected, the utility matrix obtained is sparse, fill
the unknown values with 0
print("Shape of Utility
Matrix:\n",ratings_utility_matrix.shape)

#Transposing the matrix
X = ratings_utility_matrix.T
print("Transposed Matrix:\n",X.head())
print("Transposed Matrix Shape:",X.shape)

#Unique products in subset of data
X1 = X

#Decomposing the Matrix
SVD = TruncatedSVD(n_components=10)
decomposed_matrix = SVD.fit_transform(X)
print("Decomposed Matrix Shape:",decomposed_matrix.shape)
#Correlation Matrix
correlation_matrix = np.corrcoef(decomposed_matrix)

'''
Isolating Product ID # 9601403787 from the Correlation
Matrix
Assuming the customer buys Product ID # 9601403787
(randomly chosen)
'''
print("randomly choosen Product ID: ",X.index[99])
```

```
#Index # of product ID purchased by customer
i = "9601403787"

product_names = list(X.index)
product_ID = product_names.index(i)
print("Product ID = ",product_ID)

'''
Correlation for all items with the item purchased by this
customer based on items rated by other customers people
who bought the same product
'''

correlation_product_ID = correlation_matrix[product_ID]

#Recommending top 10 highly correlated products in
sequence
Recommend = list(X.index[correlation_product_ID > 0.90])

# Removes the item already bought by the customer
Recommend.remove(i)

print("Top 10 Products Recommendation:\n",Recommend[0:9])
```
Top 10 Products Recommendation:

['130414643X', '1304651088', '130465110X', '322700075X', '3227001055', '360211600X', '4057362886', '4057362894', '4057368825']

The Product IDs mentioned above are the top 10 products to be displayed by the recommendation system to the above customer based on the purchase history of other customers on the website.

Recommendation System - Part III: For a business without any user-item purchase history

A search engine-based recommendation system can be designed for users. The product recommendations can be based on textual clustering analysis in the product description.

We will be using **TfidfVectorizer** in this program. The **TfidfVectorizer** from Python's Scikit-learn library is a tool that transforms text data into numerical features suitable for use in machine learning models, specifically those dealing with natural language processing (NLP). The acronym TF-IDF stands for "Term Frequency-Inverse

Document Frequency," a statistical measure used to evaluate the importance of a word to a document in a collection or corpus of documents.

```python
# Importing libraries

from sklearn.feature_extraction.text import
TfidfVectorizer, CountVectorizer
from sklearn.neighbors import NearestNeighbors
from sklearn.cluster import KMeans
from sklearn.metrics import adjusted_rand_score
import pandas as pd
import matplotlib.pyplot as plt
'''
Item to item based recommendation system based on product
description Applicable when business is setting up its E-
commerce website for the first time
'''
product_descriptions =
pd.read_csv('D:/datasets/akularetailrevolution/product_de
scriptions.csv')
print("Shape of the dataset:
",product_descriptions.shape)

#Checking for missing values
product_descriptions = product_descriptions.dropna()
print("Shape of the dataset after dropping missing
values: ",product_descriptions.shape)
print("Dataset:\n",product_descriptions.head())


'''
Feature extraction from product descriptions: Converting
the text in product description into numerical data for
analysis
'''
vectorizer = TfidfVectorizer(stop_words='english')
X1 =
vectorizer.fit_transform(product_descriptions["product_de
scription"])
print("Data converted to numerical format:\n",X1)

#Visualizing product clusters in subset of data
# Fitting K-Means to the dataset
X=X1
kmeans = KMeans(n_clusters = 10, init = 'k-means++')
```

```python
y_kmeans = kmeans.fit_predict(X)
plt.plot(y_kmeans, ".")
plt.show()

#Top words in each cluster based on product description
# # Optimal clusters is

true_k = 10
model = KMeans(n_clusters=true_k, init='k-means++',
max_iter=100, n_init=1)
model.fit(X1)

def print_cluster(i):
    print("Cluster %d:" % i),
    for ind in order_centroids[i, :10]:
        print(' %s' % terms[ind]),
    print()
'''
Output:
1. Recommendation of product based on the current product
selected by user.
2. To recommend related product based on, Frequently
bought together.
'''
print("Top terms per cluster:")
order_centroids = model.cluster_centers_.argsort()[:, ::-
1]
terms = vectorizer.get_feature_names_out()
for i in range(true_k):
    print_cluster(i)

## ####
# Predicting clusters based on key search words
def show_recommendations(product):
    #print("Cluster ID:")
    Y = vectorizer.transform([product])
    prediction = model.predict(Y)
    print_cluster(prediction[0])

# Keyword : cutting tool
print("Showing recommendations for cutting tool
product:")
show_recommendations("cutting tool")
```

```
'''
In case a word appears in multiple clusters, the
algorithm chooses the cluster with the highest frequency
of occurance of the word.
'''
print("Showing recommendations for water:")
show_recommendations("water")
```

```
Showing recommendations for water:
Cluster 8:
 water
 pvc
 pipe
 valve
 pressure
 faucet
 shower
 brass
 drain
 flow
```

Once a cluster is identified based on the user's search words, the recommendation system can display items from the corresponding product clusters based on the product description.

CASE STUDIES ON SUCCESSFUL IMPLEMENTATION

CASE STUDY 1: AMAZON

Overview

Amazon's recommendation system is a cornerstone of its e-commerce empire, influencing up to 35% of its total sales. By integrating complex machine learning algorithms, Amazon provides highly personalized recommendations that enhance user experience and increase sales.

How It Works

Amazon's recommendation engine employs collaborative filtering, natural language processing, and deep learning to create a personalized shopping experience:

- Collaborative Filtering: Amazon uses item-to-item collaborative filtering, which scales efficiently to massive datasets and millions of users. The system matches each user and their previously rated items to similar items and then combines those similar items into a recommendation list.

- **Content-Based Methods:** It analyzes the descriptions of the items previously purchased or rated by a user and generates recommendations for items with similar descriptions.

- **Seasonality and Trends:** Amazon's algorithms adjust recommendations based on trending products, seasonal items, and new releases that match user preferences.

- **Contextual Data:** The system also considers contextual information such as the time of day, whether the user is on a mobile device, and even current inventory levels.

Impact

The personalized recommendations encourage larger order sizes by showing users items they might need but hadn't thought of, effectively increasing the average cart value. Additionally, these tailored suggestions improve customer satisfaction by making the shopping process easier and more relevant.

CASE STUDY 2: NETFLIX

Overview

Netflix's recommendation system is critical to its business model, given it invests billions in content and needs to ensure that such content reaches the right audience. Approximately 80% of the content streamed on Netflix comes from recommendations.

How It Works

Netflix's recommendation engine uses a mixture of collaborative filtering, content-based filtering, and machine learning algorithms that consider hundreds of factors:

- **Viewing Patterns:** It monitors the shows and movies a user watches, when they watch them, and how often they pause, rewind, or fast forward.

- **Similar Users:** Netflix looks at other users with similar viewing habits to recommend shows and movies that those users liked but the current user hasn't seen yet.

- **Additional Metadata:** The algorithms consider metadata such as genres, categories, actors, release dates, and even the time of day when shows are typically watched.

- A/B Testing: Netflix constantly tests and modifies its algorithms based on how well different groups of users respond to different formats of recommendations.

Impact

This personalized approach helps Netflix keep users engaged for longer periods, reducing churn and increasing the likelihood of subscription renewals. It also ensures high viewership for new shows, justifying their production costs.

CASE STUDY 3: SPOTIFY

Overview

Spotify's Discover Weekly is a highly personalized playlist generated every week for each of its users. This feature has become a defining aspect of Spotify's service, differentiating it in a competitive streaming market.

How It Works

Spotify combines collaborative filtering and deep learning to analyze both user behavior and acoustic features of the music:

- Collaborative Filtering: By comparing user profiles and their playlists, Spotify identifies tracks that might appeal to users with similar tastes.

- Audio Analysis: Spotify employs deep learning models to understand the music itself—analyzing aspects like tempo, key, instruments used, and dynamics.

- User Interaction Data: Every skip, play, like, and playlist add is taken into account to refine and improve the recommendation accuracy continuously.

Impact

Discover Weekly not only keeps users engaged by constantly introducing them to new music but also encourages deeper platform engagement as users explore beyond their usual listening habits. This feature has helped Spotify increase user retention and satisfaction.

Each of these companies leverages sophisticated data analytics and machine learning to offer highly personalized experiences that not only meet but often exceed user expectations, driving engagement, **satisfaction, and ultimately, business success.**

CONCLUSION

Product recommendation systems are a cornerstone of AI-driven e-commerce strategies. By intelligently analyzing data to understand consumer preferences, these systems create win-win scenarios: customers enjoy a personalized shopping experience, and businesses see increased engagement and sales. As machine learning technology evolves, so will the sophistication of these systems, continually enhancing their ability to predict and meet consumer desires. Integrating these systems into e-commerce platforms represents a critical frontier in the quest for delivering superior and engaging consumer experiences.

Challenges in Product Recommendation

- **Scalability:** Managing a vast amount of data and providing real-time recommendations to millions of users is computationally intensive.
- **Cold Start:** How to provide relevant recommendations to new users or for new products that have little to no historical data.
- **Diversity and Serendipity:** Ensuring that the recommendation system does not only recommend similar items but also introduces variety and occasional surprises that might be of interest to the user.
- **Privacy and Security:** Handling personal and behavioral data responsibly to protect user privacy.

Product recommendation systems are a dynamic field that combines advanced AI technologies, detailed data analysis, and strategic marketing. As AI technology evolves and consumer data grows, these systems will become even more sophisticated, further transforming the retail landscape by making shopping experiences more personalized, efficient, and enjoyable.

* * *

CHAPTER 3

CUSTOMER BEHAVIOR ANALYSIS

Understanding customer behavior is crucial for any business looking to succeed in the highly competitive retail market. This chapter delves into how machine learning and predictive analytics are employed to analyze and predict customer behaviors and trends. We explore the mechanisms enabling businesses to understand past consumer actions and forecast future behaviors, enhancing customer engagement and satisfaction.

THE IMPORTANCE OF CUSTOMER BEHAVIOR ANALYSIS

In retail and e-commerce, customer behavior analysis is critical to drive decision-making and strategic planning. By analyzing patterns in customer data, businesses can identify what influences purchasing decisions, how different segments interact with their products, and what strategies can enhance customer retention.

Customer behavior analysis is a methodical approach that examines how consumers interact with a business across various channels and touchpoints. It encompasses the study of how and why customers make purchasing decisions, what influences their buying patterns, and how they respond to marketing strategies, both online and offline. This analysis helps businesses gain deeper insights into customer preferences and behaviors, enabling them to effectively tailor their marketing, sales, and service strategies.

Customer behavior analysis is a crucial aspect of retail management that provides insights into how customers interact with a brand across various touchpoints. By understanding customer behaviors, preferences, and purchasing patterns, retailers can optimize their strategies to improve sales, enhance customer satisfaction, and foster loyalty. Here are the key reasons why customer behavior analysis is indispensable in retail management:

1. Enhanced Personalization

Analyzing customer behavior allows retailers to personalize the shopping experience in ways that resonate deeply with each individual. Personalization can range from targeted marketing and promotions to personalized product recommendations and online or in-store shopping experiences. This level of personalization increases the likelihood of purchases and enhances customer satisfaction and loyalty.

2. Improved Product Assortment

Customer behavior analysis helps retailers understand which products are popular, trending, or underperforming. This knowledge enables them to adjust their product assortments and stock levels more effectively, ensuring that popular products are readily available while minimizing excess inventory of less popular items. Retailers can also identify potential gaps in their offerings and introduce new products that meet emerging customer needs.

3. Optimized Pricing Strategies

Understanding how customers react to different pricing strategies can significantly impact a retailer's ability to compete in the market. Behavior analysis provides insights into customer price sensitivity, which can guide dynamic pricing strategies, promotions, and discounts. Retailers can optimize prices to maximize sales volume and profit margins based on how price changes affect customer buying behavior.

4. Effective Marketing and Promotions

Retailers can design more effective marketing campaigns and promotional strategies by analyzing customer behavior. Insights into customer preferences and behaviors allow for the creation of targeted marketing efforts more likely to resonate with specific customer segments. Additionally, understanding the effectiveness of previous marketing strategies through behavior analysis helps retailers refine their approach, ensuring that future campaigns are more focused and cost-effective.

5. Enhanced Customer Experiences

Analyzing customer interactions across different channels (online, mobile, and in-store) provides a comprehensive view of the customer journey. Retailers can use this information to streamline processes, reduce friction points, and ensure a seamless shopping experience. Improving customer experience is crucial for increasing customer retention and converting one-time buyers into loyal customers.

6. Strategic Decision Making

Customer behavior insights drive strategic decision-making in areas beyond marketing and sales, including store layout, staff allocation, and even the selection of store locations. By understanding where, when, and how customers prefer to shop, retailers can make informed decisions that align with customer preferences and operational goals.

7. Predicting Future Trends

With advanced analytics and predictive modeling, retailers can forecast future buying trends and behaviors based on historical data. This proactive approach allows retailers to stay ahead of the curve, adapting to changes in consumer preferences and market conditions before they become apparent.

8. Improving Customer Retention

Behavior analysis helps identify patterns that may indicate customer churn, such as decreased frequency of purchases or reduced engagement with marketing communications. By recognizing these signs early, retailers can implement targeted retention strategies to re-engage at-risk customers.

Key Components of Customer Behavior Analysis

1. Data Collection

The foundation of customer behavior analysis is data. This includes:

- **Transactional Data**: Records of every purchase, including what was bought, when, and for how much.

- **Engagement Data**: Interactions with the brand through various channels such as websites, mobile apps, and social media platforms, including clicks, views, and comments or likes.

- **Demographic Data**: Information about the customer's age, gender, income level, education, and more, which can help in segmenting the customer base.

- **Psychographic Data**: Preferences, lifestyles, and attitudes influencing buying decisions.

2. Data Analysis

Once data is collected, it is next analyzed to extract meaningful insights. Techniques used include:

- **Statistical Analysis**: To find trends and patterns in the data.
- **Predictive Modeling**: To forecast future behaviors based on past patterns.
- **Segmentation**: Grouping customers with similar behaviors or traits for more targeted marketing.
- **Customer Journey Mapping**: Visualizing customers' path from learning about a product to purchasing.

3. Implementation of Insights

The insights gained from customer behavior analysis are applied to:

- **Personalize Marketing Messages**: Tailoring messages to meet the specific needs and desires of different segments.

- **Optimize the Product Portfolio**: Adjusting product offerings based on what different segments of customers prefer or need.

- **Enhance Customer Experience**: Streamlining processes and eliminating pain points along the customer journey to improve satisfaction and loyalty.

- **Pricing Strategy**: Develop pricing strategies that match what different customer segments are willing to pay.

Techniques Used in Customer Behavior Analysis

- **A/B Testing**: Comparing two versions of a webpage, app, or campaign to see which performs better and understand customer preferences.

- **Machine Learning**: Using algorithms to predict future behavior based on past data.

- **Heatmaps**: Visual tools that show where customers click, scroll, and spend time on a website.

- **Sentiment Analysis**: Using natural language processing to understand customer sentiments from reviews, social media posts, and customer support interactions.

Challenges in Customer Behavior Analysis

- **Data Privacy and Security**: Ensuring customer data is collected, stored, and processed in compliance with privacy laws and ethical standards.

- **Data Silos**: Difficulty in integrating data from various sources can lead to incomplete views of customer behavior.

- **Changing Consumer Behaviors**: Consumer preferences and behaviors can change rapidly, making it challenging to keep analysis current and relevant.

USING MACHINE LEARNING TO PREDICT CUSTOMER BEHAVIORS

Machine Learning (ML) can be a powerful tool to predict customer behaviors by analyzing patterns in historical data. These predictions can inform decisions related to marketing, sales, product development, and customer retention strategies. Here's an example of how a fitness device manufacturing company could use machine learning to predict customer behaviors:

Scenario: Predicting Customer Churn for a Fitness Device Company

Business Problem:

A fitness device company sells smart fitness devices (such as wearables, smart scales, and fitness trackers) and offers monthly subscriptions for additional services like personalized workout plans and health monitoring. Recently, the company has noticed an increase in **customer churn** (customers canceling their subscriptions), which impacts revenue and growth. The company wants to predict which customers are likely to churn so it can take proactive measures to retain them.

Objective:

Use machine learning to predict which customers are likely to cancel their subscription within the next three months, allowing the company to target at-risk customers with retention campaigns.

Step 1: Collect and Prepare Data

The first step is to collect historical customer data that might be indicative of customer churn. This could include:

1. **Customer Demographics:**

    o   Age

    o   Gender

    o   Location

    o   Income level

2. **Customer Engagement Data:**

    o   Usage frequency of the fitness device (e.g., workouts per week, number of steps tracked)

    o   Usage of mobile app features (e.g., checking workout history, health metrics, etc.)

    o   Participation in fitness challenges or community features

    o   Frequency of syncing data between the device and the app

3. **Subscription Details:**

    o   Subscription start date

    o   Subscription renewal/cancellation history

    o   Subscription plan type (e.g., basic, premium)

    o   Payment history and billing frequency

4. **Customer Support Interactions:**

    o   Number of support tickets raised

    o   Response time to support queries

- o   Customer satisfaction score

5. **Marketing Data:**

   - o   Responses to promotional emails

   - o   Engagement with social media ads or campaigns

6. **Churn Labels:**

   - o   Whether the customer churned (Yes/No)

Goal:

Label the historical data with the outcome (whether the customer churned or not) to create a **training dataset** for the machine learning model.

Step 2: Choose and Prepare Features

The next step is to select relevant **features** (inputs) that will help predict whether a customer will churn. Examples of key features might include:

- Number of workouts completed in the last 30 days

- Decline in workout frequency over the last three months

- Subscription plan type (basic vs. premium)

- Number of customer support tickets in the last 6 months

- Interaction with marketing emails (clicks or opens)

- Frequency of app use (daily, weekly, etc.)

Feature Engineering:

In some cases, new features can be created by combining or transforming existing ones. For instance, creating a feature called **"workout frequency trend"** that captures changes in workout frequency over time might be more predictive than simply looking at the number of workouts completed.

Step 3: Select and Train the Machine Learning Model

Several machine learning algorithms can be used to predict customer churn. Some common models for this type of classification problem include:

- **Logistic Regression:** A basic and interpretable model that predicts the probability of churn based on customer features.

- **Decision Trees:** A model that splits data based on certain features to classify whether a customer will churn or not.

- **Random Forest:** An ensemble method that builds multiple decision trees to improve prediction accuracy.

- **Gradient Boosting Machines (GBM):** A powerful ensemble method that combines weak models to improve performance.

- **XGBoost/LightGBM:** Advanced versions of gradient boosting that are optimized for speed and performance.

Example: We decide to use a **Random Forest Classifier** for our churn prediction. This model will evaluate all the selected features and identify patterns that distinguish churned customers from those who stayed.

Training the Model:

Split the dataset into a **training set** (to train the model) and a **test set** (to evaluate its performance). Typically, 70-80% of the data is used for training, and 20-30% for testing. The model will learn from the training data and make predictions about whether a customer will churn.

Step 4: Model Evaluation and Tuning

After training the model, evaluate its performance using metrics such as:

- **Accuracy:** The percentage of correctly predicted outcomes (churn or no churn).

- **Precision:** The percentage of true churn predictions out of all predicted churn cases (i.e., how many predicted churns were actual churns).

- **Recall:** The percentage of actual churn cases that were correctly identified by the model (i.e., how many real churners were caught by the model).

- **F1 Score:** The harmonic mean of precision and recall, used to balance the two metrics.

For example:

- **Accuracy = 85%** (the model correctly predicts whether a customer churns 85% of the time).

- **Precision = 78%** (78% of customers predicted to churn actually churned).

- **Recall = 80%** (the model correctly identified 80% of the customers who churned).

If the model underperforms, **hyperparameter tuning** (e.g., adjusting the depth of decision trees or the number of trees in the random forest) can improve its accuracy.

Step 5: Predict and Take Action

Once the model performs well, use it to predict churn for **current customers** who are still subscribed. The model assigns a probability score to each customer, indicating how likely they are to churn.

Example:

Customer A has a **churn probability of 0.85** (85% chance of canceling), while Customer B has a **churn probability of 0.15** (15% chance of canceling).

Based on these predictions, the company can:

1. **Target High-Risk Customers (e.g., Customer A) with Retention Campaigns:**

    o Offer personalized incentives such as discounts, free upgrades, or personalized workout plans.

    o Reach out with personalized emails or customer service calls to address potential concerns.

2. **Monitor Low-Risk Customers (e.g., Customer B):**

    o Continue to offer general engagement tactics to maintain their loyalty, without needing to invest in costly retention efforts.

Step 6: Continuous Improvement

The machine learning model should not remain static. Continuously retrain and update the model using the most recent customer data to improve accuracy over time. If new features become available (such as engagement with new app features), they should be incorporated into the model.

Feedback Loop:

Use the outcomes of retention campaigns (whether customers stayed or churned) as feedback to improve the predictive model. This helps fine-tune the model's ability to predict future churn more accurately.

Program: Customer Churn Prediction

```
# Import necessary libraries
import pandas as pd
from sklearn.model_selection import train_test_split
from sklearn.ensemble import RandomForestClassifier
from sklearn.preprocessing import LabelEncoder
from sklearn.metrics import accuracy_score,
classification_report, confusion_matrix
```

```
df =
pd.read_csv("D:/datasets/akularetailrevolution/customer_c
hurn_data.csv")

# Data preprocessing: Encode categorical variables
label_encoders = {}
for column in ['Gender', 'Location', 'IncomeLevel',
'AppUsageFrequency', 'SubscriptionPlan',
'PaymentHistory']:
    le = LabelEncoder()
    df[column] = le.fit_transform(df[column])
    label_encoders[column] = le

# Split the data into features (X) and target (y)
X = df.drop(columns=['CustomerID', 'Churn'])  # Features
(excluding customer ID and churn label)
y = df['Churn']  # Target (churn label)

# Split the dataset into training and test sets
X_train, X_test, y_train, y_test = train_test_split(X, y,
test_size=0.3, random_state=42)

# Initialize and train the Random Forest Classifier
rf_model = RandomForestClassifier(n_estimators=100,
random_state=42)
rf_model.fit(X_train, y_train)

# Predict on the test set
y_pred = rf_model.predict(X_test)

# Evaluate the model
accuracy = accuracy_score(y_test, y_pred)
classification_rep = classification_report(y_test,
y_pred)
conf_matrix = confusion_matrix(y_test, y_pred)

# Output model evaluation results
print(f"Accuracy: {accuracy * 100:.2f}%")
print("\nClassification Report:\n", classification_rep)
print("\nConfusion Matrix:\n", conf_matrix)
```

OUTPUT:

```
Classification Report:
              precision    recall  f1-score   support

           0       0.65      0.98      0.78       195
           1       0.33      0.02      0.04       105

    accuracy                           0.64       300
   macro avg       0.49      0.50      0.41       300
weighted avg       0.54      0.64      0.52       300
```

```
Confusion Matrix:
 [[191    4]
  [103    2]]
```

Insights:

The model performs reasonably well in identifying customers who did not churn (precision and recall are high for class 0), but it struggles with identifying customers who churned (class 1).

This imbalance may be due to the relatively smaller number of churned customers in the dataset, suggesting that further tuning, resampling techniques (like SMOTE), or feature engineering may be needed to improve performance on churn prediction.

Next Steps:

If you'd like to improve the model, you can explore feature engineering, hyperparameter tuning, or rebalancing the dataset to address the imbalance between churned and non-churned customers.

Key Benefits of Using Machine Learning for Predicting Customer Behaviors

1. **Proactive Action:** Predictive models allow companies to act before churn happens, helping them retain valuable customers and reduce revenue loss.

2. **Resource Optimization:** Instead of applying retention strategies to the entire customer base, machine learning helps identify and focus on high-risk customers, optimizing marketing and customer support resources.

3. **Personalization:** The insights gained from predictive analytics allow for personalized customer experiences, increasing satisfaction and reducing churn over time.

4. **Data-Driven Decisions:** Machine learning provides actionable insights from vast amounts of customer data, improving decision-making accuracy and speed.

Machine learning can significantly improve a company's ability to predict and act on customer behavior, particularly in scenarios like customer churn. In the fitness device industry, leveraging customer data (such as device usage patterns, subscription behavior, and engagement with digital services) through predictive models can help identify at-risk customers and develop targeted retention strategies, ultimately improving customer satisfaction and business growth.

UNDERSTANDING MACHINE LEARNING IN BEHAVIOR ANALYSIS

Machine learning offers advanced capabilities beyond traditional statistical methods, enabling more accurate predictions and deeper insights into customer behavior. These models can identify subtle patterns and correlations that might not be evident to human analysts.

Key Techniques

1. **Classification Models:** Predict categorical outcomes, such as whether a customer will buy a product. Algorithms like logistic regression, decision trees, and support vector machines are commonly used.

2. **Regression Models:** Employed when predicting a continuous outcome, such as how much a customer will spend. Linear regression and its derivatives are typically utilized.

3. **Clustering Techniques:** Useful for segmenting customers into groups based on similar behaviors or preferences. Algorithms like K-means or hierarchical clustering help tailor marketing strategies to each segment.

4. **Sequence Analysis:** Helps in predicting the sequence of products a customer might buy, which is particularly useful in markets like fashion or technology.

Leveraging Predictive Analytics for Customer Engagement

Predictive analytics uses historical data, statistical algorithms, and machine learning techniques to predict future outcomes. Customer behavior analysis is pivotal in enhancing customer engagement and satisfaction by foreseeing and effectively responding to customer needs and trends. Predictive analytics has become an essential tool for enhancing customer engagement by enabling businesses to anticipate customer needs, personalize interactions, and optimize their services. This tutorial will guide you through the steps of leveraging predictive analytics for customer engagement, from data collection to actionable insights.

Step 1: Understanding Predictive Analytics

Predictive analytics uses historical data, machine learning algorithms, and statistical techniques to predict future outcomes based on patterns identified in the data. In the context of customer engagement, it helps anticipate customer behaviors, preferences, and potential churn, which can be critical for tailoring marketing strategies and enhancing customer experiences.

Step 2: Data Collection

The first step in leveraging predictive analytics is gathering the necessary data. Effective predictive models are built on comprehensive, high-quality data. Key data types include:

- **Transactional Data:** Records of customer purchases, returns, and interactions that provide insights into buying behavior and product preferences.

- **Behavioral Data:** Data from website visits, app usage, and social media interactions that help understand how customers engage with your brand online.

- **Demographic Data:** Information about the customer's age, gender, location, income level, and more, which can be used for segmentation.

- **Feedback Data:** Customer feedback and survey responses provide direct insights into customer satisfaction and areas for improvement.

Step 3: Data Preparation

Data needs to be cleaned and prepared before it can be used for modeling:

- **Cleaning Data:** Address missing values, remove duplicates, and correct inconsistencies.

- **Feature Engineering:** Create new variables that might be predictive of customer behavior, such as customer lifetime value, average transaction size, or frequency of interaction.

- **Data Transformation:** Normalize or scale data if necessary to prepare for machine learning algorithms.

Step 4: Choosing the Right Model

Selecting the right predictive model depends on the specific business goal. Common models include:

- **Regression Models:** Useful for predicting quantities, like how much a customer will spend.

- **Classification Models:** Suitable for predicting categorical outcomes, such as whether a customer will churn.

- **Clustering Models:** Ideal for segmenting customers into groups based on similar behaviors or characteristics.

Step 5: Model Training and Validation

- **Training the Model:** Use historical data to train your predictive model. This involves splitting the data into training and testing sets to ensure the model can generalize well to new data.

- **Model Validation:** Use metrics such as accuracy, precision, recall, and AUC-ROC curve to evaluate the performance of your model. Adjust parameters and try different algorithms if necessary to improve the model.

Step 6: Implementation and Testing

- **Integration:** Deploy the model into your business processes, integrating it with your CRM and marketing automation tools.

- **Real-time Analytics:** Use the model to score customer behaviors in real-time and trigger actions like sending a personalized offer when a customer is predicted to churn.

Step 7: Continuous Learning and Improvement

- **Feedback Loop:** Continuously feed new customer data back into the model to refine and improve its predictions over time.

- **Monitor Performance:** Regularly check the performance of your predictive models and update them as needed to adapt to changes in customer behavior and market conditions.

Step 8: Actionable Insights

Use the insights from your predictive models to enhance customer engagement:

- **Personalized Marketing:** Tailor marketing messages and offers based on predicted customer preferences and behaviors.

- **Proactive Customer Service:** Anticipate issues and reach out to customers before they contact support.

- **Optimized Product Recommendations:** Improve cross-selling and upselling by recommending products that the customer is likely to be interested in based on predictive analytics.

Applications of Predictive Analytics

1. **Personalized Marketing:** Predictive models can determine the most effective marketing strategies for different customer segments, predicting what offers or promotions a customer will likely respond to based on their past behavior.

2. **Customer Churn Prevention:** By predicting which customers are at risk of churn, businesses can proactively engage these customers with targeted retention strategies, personalized offers, or loyalty rewards.

3. **Product Recommendations:** Similar to recommendation systems discussed earlier, predictive analytics can be fine-tuned to predict what new products a customer might be interested in based on their past purchases and browsing behavior.

4. **Optimizing Customer Journey:** By predicting and understanding the pain points in the customer journey, companies can implement changes to enhance the overall customer experience, thus boosting satisfaction and loyalty.

CASE STUDIES ON EFFECTIVE CUSTOMER BEHAVIOR ANALYSIS

CASE STUDY 1: TARGET

Target, a leading retailer in the United States, implemented sophisticated predictive analytics capabilities to understand and predict customer behaviors. One of the most notable applications has been its ability to predict major life events, such as pregnancy, based on shopping patterns.

Methodology

Target developed models that analyze purchasing patterns to predict customer life changes. For example, they found that when customers start buying unscented lotion, supplements like calcium, magnesium, and zinc, or extra-large bags of cotton balls, they might be in the early stages of pregnancy. These predictive models are based on the analysis of historical buying data correlated with life events that were self-reported by customers in other marketing channels (such as baby registry sign-ups).

Application and Results

With this information, Target could send coupons tailored to the pregnancy stage and other baby-related products, effectively targeting consumers at a crucial decision-making phase. This predictive targeting approach increased customer spending at Target stores, particularly in the baby and child product segments.

Challenges

The program, while successful, also faced criticism when it inadvertently revealed a teen girl's pregnancy to her family before she had disclosed it. This incident highlighted the potential privacy concerns and the ethical considerations companies must manage when using predictive analytics.

CASE STUDY 2: UBER

Uber uses machine learning extensively to optimize its ride-sharing services. By analyzing vast amounts of data on rider demand, traffic patterns, and other variables, Uber can predict demand in different areas and adjust its supply of drivers accordingly.

Methodology

Uber employs various machine learning algorithms to predict where and when high ride demand will occur. This involves analyzing historical data related to rider usage patterns, events in the city, weather conditions, and even factors like the day of the week and time of day.

Application and Results

The predictive insights allow Uber to implement dynamic pricing, which adjusts ride prices in real time based on the predicted demand. This helps balance rider demand and driver supply, reducing wait times for riders and increasing effective earnings for drivers by strategically positioning them in high-demand areas. This responsiveness to customer demand enhances overall user satisfaction and operational efficiency.

Challenges

While effective, dynamic pricing can sometimes lead to public relations challenges, such as when prices surge dramatically due to extraordinary events, sometimes catching riders by surprise.

CASE STUDY 3: NETFLIX

Netflix employs sophisticated behavior analysis to recommend content to viewers and inform its decisions regarding original content production and acquisition.

Methodology

Netflix collects detailed data on viewing habits, such as what shows are watched, when they are watched, and how often they are paused or rewatched. By analyzing this data, Netflix can identify patterns and trends in viewer preferences and predict future viewing behaviors.

Application and Results

The insights gained from behavior analysis help Netflix decide which types of shows and movies to produce or acquire. This targeted content strategy ensures high engagement rates by aligning new productions with proven user preferences, thus keeping the audience engaged and subscribed. For example, the success of original series like "Stranger Things" and "The Crown" was backed by behavior analysis that indicated a strong viewer interest in these genres and themes.

Challenges

Netflix faces the challenge of maintaining user privacy and trust as the company handles sensitive data on viewing preferences. There is also the ongoing challenge of adapting to rapidly changing viewer tastes and the increasing competition in the streaming content industry.

These case studies exemplify how effective customer behavior analysis can significantly enhance strategic decision-making and operational efficiency in diverse industries. By leveraging data to understand and predict customer behaviors, companies like Target, Uber, and Netflix can tailor their offerings to meet customer needs more precisely, thereby enhancing satisfaction and loyalty. However, these approaches also necessitate careful consideration of ethical and privacy concerns to maintain trust and compliance with regulations.

CONCLUSION

The analysis and prediction of customer behaviors through machine learning and predictive analytics represent a powerful toolset for modern businesses. These technologies allow companies to stay ahead, anticipate customer needs and trends, and respond in real-time with personalized, relevant interactions. As these tools evolve, so will the sophistication with which businesses can cater to their customers, ultimately enhancing the customer experience and driving business success. This proactive approach to customer behavior analysis is no longer just advantageous—it's essential for any business looking to thrive in the digital age.

* * *

UNIT

2

OPERATIONAL
EFFICIENCY
AND
OPTIMIZATION

CHAPTER 4

INVENTORY MANAGEMENT

Effective inventory management is crucial for the success of retail operations, as it directly impacts customer satisfaction, operational efficiency, and the financial health of a business. This chapter explores how predictive models and machine learning are revolutionizing inventory management by enabling more accurate demand forecasting and optimization of the supply chain.

The Importance of Inventory Management

In the retail sector, inventory management involves overseeing the flow of goods from manufacturers to warehouses and from these facilities to point of sale. The main challenge lies in maintaining the right balance—having enough inventory to meet customer demand without overstocking or understocking. Advanced inventory management using machine learning not only addresses this balance but also enhances operational efficiencies and reduces waste.

USING PREDICTIVE MODELS TO FORECAST DEMAND

Overview of Predictive Modeling

Predictive modeling uses historical data and analytics to make informed predictions about future outcomes. In inventory management, these models forecast product demand based on various factors such as seasonal trends, market conditions, and consumer behavior patterns.

Techniques in Demand Forecasting

1. **Time Series Analysis:** Utilizes methods like ARIMA (AutoRegressive Integrated Moving Average) to forecast future demand based on past sales data.
2. **Regression Models:** These models predict demand based on a range of independent variables, from marketing activities to economic indicators.
3. **Machine Learning Algorithms:** More complex algorithms, such as Random Forests and Gradient Boosting Machines, can detect non-linear relationships and interactions between predictors, providing more accurate forecasts.

Implementing Predictive Demand Forecasting
- **Data Collection:** Gather historical sales data, promotional calendars, external factors like weather or economic indicators.
- **Model Selection and Training:** Choose the appropriate model based on the data characteristics and business objectives. Train the model with historical data to learn patterns.
- **Validation and Testing:** Regularly validate the model against recent data to ensure its accuracy and make adjustments as needed.

OPTIMIZING SUPPLY CHAIN WITH MACHINE LEARNING AND ARTIFICIAL INTELLIGENCE

Inventory management is a crucial function for retailers, as it directly affects customer satisfaction, operational efficiency, and the bottom line. The challenge lies in balancing supply and demand—having enough stock to meet customer demand without overstocking, which leads to increased holding costs and potential waste. Artificial Intelligence (AI) has revolutionized how retailers manage their inventory, enabling more accurate demand forecasting, automated replenishment, real-time insights, and optimization of supply chains.

1. Demand Forecasting with AI

One of the most critical aspects of inventory management is predicting customer demand. Traditional methods often use historical sales data or simple trend analysis, but AI can take demand forecasting to the next level by analyzing complex patterns, trends, and external factors.

How AI Improves Demand Forecasting:
- **Machine Learning Models:** AI-powered machine learning models can analyze vast amounts of data, including historical sales, customer behavior, seasonality, promotions, competitor activities, economic indicators, and weather patterns. These models can predict future demand more accurately than traditional methods.
- **Time-Series Forecasting:** Advanced algorithms such as ARIMA, Prophet, or Long Short-Term Memory (LSTM) networks can be applied to time-series data (e.g., sales over time) to forecast future sales trends and help retailers plan inventory levels.
- **Dynamic Forecasting:** AI can generate dynamic, real-time demand forecasts, which can be updated as new data comes in, allowing retailers to adjust inventory levels proactively.

Example of Demand Forecasting Using AI:

A large retail chain uses machine learning models to predict how many units of a popular fitness tracker will be sold in the next quarter. The model considers:

- Historical sales data.
- Upcoming promotions and marketing campaigns.
- Seasonal spikes in fitness equipment demand after New Year (due to fitness resolutions).
- Economic factors affecting consumer spending.

Based on the AI-generated forecast, the retailer can adjust its procurement orders to avoid stockouts or excess inventory.

2. Inventory Optimization and Stock Levels

AI can help retailers optimize stock levels by calculating the **optimal reorder points** and **safety stock levels** for each product. This ensures that products are available when needed while minimizing overstock and holding costs.

How AI Optimizes Inventory Levels:

- **Reorder Point Calculation:** AI systems can analyze sales velocity, lead times, and supplier reliability to determine the optimal reorder point—the inventory level at which new stock should be ordered. The AI takes into account variability in demand and supply chain disruptions.
- **Safety Stock Calculation:** AI algorithms dynamically adjust safety stock levels based on factors such as demand fluctuations, delivery lead time variability, and seasonality. Retailers can maintain a buffer of stock to protect against unexpected demand spikes or supplier delays.
- **Just-In-Time Inventory (JIT):** AI helps retailers implement just-in-time inventory management by predicting when stock should arrive, minimizing storage costs, and reducing the risk of overstock.

Example of AI-Driven Inventory Optimization:

An e-commerce retailer uses AI to calculate reorder points for each product. By analyzing historical sales patterns, supplier lead times, and potential risks (e.g., shipping delays), the system determines that the retailer should reorder a popular product when there are 50 units left in stock. AI also suggests keeping a safety stock of 20 units to cover potential spikes in demand.

3. Automated Replenishment

AI enables **automated replenishment systems** that can autonomously trigger purchase orders when stock levels fall below a certain threshold. By integrating AI into the supply chain and warehouse management systems, retailers can ensure that stock is replenished before it runs out.

How AI Enables Automated Replenishment:
- **Autonomous Purchase Orders:** AI monitors stock levels in real-time and automatically generates purchase orders when inventory drops below the reorder point. The system accounts for supplier lead times and upcoming demand to avoid over-ordering or under-ordering.
- **Dynamic Reordering:** AI adjusts reorder quantities based on real-time data and forecasts, allowing retailers to respond flexibly to changes in demand or supply chain conditions.

Example of AI-Powered Automated Replenishment:
A supermarket chain implements an AI-driven system that automatically replenishes products based on current inventory levels and forecasted demand. When the stock of a popular cereal brand drops to a predefined threshold, the system automatically generates a purchase order and sends it to the supplier, ensuring a seamless restocking process.

4. Inventory Visibility and Real-Time Monitoring
AI, combined with Internet of Things (IoT) sensors and RFID tags, enables real-time inventory visibility across all channels, including stores, warehouses, and distribution centers. Retailers can monitor stock levels and product movement in real time, allowing for faster decision-making.

How AI Enhances Inventory Visibility:
- **IoT-Enabled Inventory Tracking:** By using IoT devices such as sensors, retailers can track the movement of products throughout the supply chain. AI processes this data in real time, providing insights into inventory status and product location.
- **Smart Warehousing:** AI-powered systems can optimize warehouse operations, track inventory levels in real-time, and provide insights into stock usage, product placement, and reordering needs.
- **Multi-Channel Inventory Management:** AI allows for seamless integration of inventory data across online and physical stores, ensuring that customers and retailers have visibility into product availability across all locations.

Example of AI-Driven Inventory Visibility:
A large department store chain uses AI and IoT to monitor its inventory in real time. Sensors track the location of products within the warehouse, while AI analyzes the data to provide a real-time view of stock levels across all stores and warehouses. This allows the retailer to transfer stock between locations based on demand, avoiding stockouts at popular stores and minimizing deadstock.

5. Supplier Relationship Management
AI can help retailers optimize their supply chain and improve supplier relationships by predicting supplier performance, lead times, and risks. Retailers can use AI-driven insights to manage suppliers more effectively, ensuring timely deliveries and consistent product quality.

How AI Improves Supplier Management:
- **Predictive Lead Times:** AI analyzes historical data to predict how long it will take for suppliers to deliver goods. This helps retailers better plan inventory levels and adjust for potential delays.
- **Supplier Performance Evaluation:** AI models assess supplier performance based on various metrics, such as on-time delivery, product quality, and cost efficiency. Retailers can use these insights to negotiate better contracts or switch to more reliable suppliers.
- **Risk Management:** AI can identify potential risks in the supply chain, such as geopolitical issues or disruptions caused by natural disasters, and recommend alternative suppliers or routes.

Example of AI-Enhanced Supplier Management:
An electronics retailer uses AI to analyze the performance of its suppliers. The system tracks lead times, delivery consistency, and product defect rates, providing a performance score for each supplier. Based on these insights, the retailer negotiates better terms with high-performing suppliers and diversifies its supplier base to reduce the risk of delays.

6. Minimizing Shrinkage and Theft
AI-driven **computer vision** and data analytics can help retailers reduce inventory shrinkage (loss due to theft, fraud, or administrative errors). By analyzing transaction data, camera footage, and product movements, AI systems can detect anomalies that may indicate theft or other issues.

How AI Reduces Shrinkage:

- **AI-Powered Video Surveillance:** Computer vision systems analyze CCTV footage to detect suspicious behavior, such as shoplifting or internal theft, and alert store managers in real-time.
- **Fraud Detection:** AI models analyze point-of-sale (POS) data to identify fraudulent activities, such as price manipulation or inventory mismanagement.
- **Anomaly Detection:** AI systems can detect discrepancies between physical inventory counts and system records, flagging potential shrinkage issues for further investigation.

Example of AI in Shrinkage Reduction:

A grocery chain uses AI-powered cameras to monitor store activities. The system automatically flags suspicious activities, such as a customer attempting to hide items or an employee manipulating the checkout process. AI also analyzes sales data to identify discrepancies between recorded sales and actual stock levels, helping the retailer reduce shrinkage.

7. Handling Seasonal Demand and Promotions

Retailers often face fluctuating demand during holidays, promotions, or specific seasons. AI can help predict and manage these spikes by analyzing historical data, customer behavior, and external factors.

How AI Manages Seasonal Demand:

- **Seasonality Analysis:** AI identifies seasonal trends and predicts when demand will spike for specific products. This allows retailers to stock up on seasonal items and avoid stockouts during peak periods.
- **Promotion Impact Analysis:** AI analyzes how past promotions have impacted sales and uses this data to forecast the effects of upcoming promotions, enabling better inventory planning.
- **Demand Surge Prediction:** AI models can anticipate surges in demand caused by holidays or special events (e.g., Black Friday), allowing retailers to adjust inventory levels and avoid losing sales.

Example of AI in Seasonal Inventory Management:

A fashion retailer uses AI to predict demand for winter coats based on weather forecasts, historical sales data, and upcoming holiday promotions. The system suggests increasing stock levels by 20% in November and December to meet the expected surge in demand, helping the retailer avoid stockouts during the peak shopping season.

8. Pricing and Inventory Markdowns

AI helps retailers optimize pricing strategies by analyzing demand patterns, market conditions, and inventory levels. By determining the optimal time to markdown products, AI can reduce excess inventory and maximize revenue.

How AI Optimizes Pricing:

- **Dynamic Pricing:** AI systems can adjust prices in real-time based on demand, competition, and inventory levels. For instance, as inventory levels drop, the system can increase prices to capitalize on scarcity.
- **Markdown Optimization:** AI helps retailers determine the best time and percentage for markdowns to clear excess inventory without sacrificing too much profit. By analyzing historical data on sales trends, the AI system can suggest gradual markdowns to move slow-selling products before they become obsolete.
- **Price Sensitivity Analysis:** AI can analyze how sensitive customers are to price changes for different products. Based on this analysis, it can recommend price reductions for items with high price elasticity and suggest higher markups for items with less price sensitivity.

Example of AI-Powered Pricing Optimization:

A home goods retailer uses AI to optimize pricing for its seasonal products. The system analyzes sales patterns and suggests markdowns for slow-moving products at the end of each season. For example, after the holiday season, AI suggests reducing prices for unsold Christmas decorations by 30% to clear inventory while still maintaining profitability.

9. Managing Returns and Reverse Logistics

Handling returns efficiently is essential to maintaining customer satisfaction and managing inventory costs. AI can help retailers streamline their **reverse logistics** (the process of managing returns, refurbishing, and restocking) to minimize disruptions in inventory management.

How AI Manages Returns:

- **Return Prediction:** AI can predict which products are most likely to be returned based on customer behavior, product reviews, or historical return data. Retailers can use this information to adjust their stock levels and reduce over-ordering of high-return items.

- **Optimizing Return Logistics:** AI can help automate the return process by determining the best routes for collecting and restocking returned items. It can also suggest whether returned items should be resold, refurbished, or disposed of based on their condition.
- **Improving Return Policies:** By analyzing return patterns, AI can suggest improvements to return policies, such as adjusting the return window for specific products or categories to reduce unnecessary returns.

Example of AI in Return Management:

An electronics retailer uses AI to predict which customers are most likely to return products. The system analyzes purchase history, product reviews, and previous return patterns to flag products with high return rates. This allows the retailer to adjust its inventory for these products and streamline the return process, reducing the cost of handling returns.

10. Supply Chain Risk Management

AI can help retailers identify and mitigate risks in their supply chain, such as supplier disruptions, geopolitical issues, or natural disasters. By continuously monitoring supply chain data and external factors, AI provides early warnings of potential disruptions and suggests alternatives.

How AI Improves Supply Chain Risk Management:

- **Predictive Risk Analysis:** AI models analyze data from various sources, such as weather reports, political news, and financial data, to predict potential disruptions in the supply chain. This allows retailers to act preemptively, such as securing backup suppliers or increasing safety stock.
- **Supplier Performance Monitoring:** AI tracks supplier performance over time and identifies trends in delays, quality issues, or price increases. Retailers can use these insights to optimize supplier relationships and avoid risks before they affect inventory levels.
- **Scenario Planning:** AI helps retailers simulate different supply chain scenarios (e.g., a supplier's factory shutting down) and develop contingency plans. These simulations help retailers understand how different risks will impact inventory and prepare for disruptions.

Example of AI in Supply Chain Risk Management:
A global apparel retailer uses AI to monitor its supply chain and detect potential risks. The AI system analyzes weather patterns and predicts that a hurricane is likely to disrupt one of the retailer's key suppliers. Based on this prediction, the retailer increases its stock levels for items sourced from the affected region and reaches out to alternative suppliers, minimizing the impact of the disruption.

11. Customer Insights and Personalization
AI-driven **customer insights** allow retailers to better understand their customers' preferences and buying behavior, which in turn informs inventory decisions. By analyzing customer data, AI can help retailers predict which products are likely to be in high demand, enabling more personalized inventory management strategies.

How AI Personalizes Inventory Management:
- **Customer Segmentation:** AI segments customers based on their buying habits, demographics, and preferences. Retailers can tailor their inventory to match the needs of different customer segments, ensuring that the right products are available to the right customers.
- **Product Recommendations:** AI analyzes customer purchase data to recommend products that are likely to sell well. Retailers can use these recommendations to adjust their inventory and focus on stocking high-demand items.
- **Predictive Customer Behavior:** AI models can predict how customers will respond to new products, promotions, or price changes, allowing retailers to stock inventory accordingly.

Example of AI in Customer-Centric Inventory Management:
An online fashion retailer uses AI to segment its customers into different categories based on purchasing behavior (e.g., frequent buyers, occasional buyers, budget-conscious buyers). The AI system recommends stocking more high-end fashion items for frequent buyers and promoting discounted products to budget-conscious customers. This personalized inventory management ensures that each customer segment is catered to, improving overall sales.

12. AI-Driven Sustainability in Inventory Management
Sustainability is becoming increasingly important for retailers. AI can help optimize inventory management in a way that reduces waste and minimizes environmental impact, supporting corporate sustainability goals.

How AI Supports Sustainable Inventory Management:
- **Reducing Overstock and Waste:** AI reduces overstock by accurately predicting demand and automating replenishment processes. This minimizes waste, particularly for perishable products.
- **Efficient Resource Allocation:** AI helps retailers optimize transportation routes and warehouse management, reducing energy consumption and carbon emissions in the supply chain.
- **Sustainable Sourcing:** AI analyzes supplier data to recommend sustainable sourcing options, such as environmentally friendly packaging or suppliers with lower carbon footprints.

Example of AI for Sustainable Inventory:
A grocery retailer uses AI to reduce food waste by predicting the exact demand for perishable items such as fruits and vegetables. The AI system analyzes weather patterns, local events, and historical sales data to ensure that only the necessary amount of perishable goods is ordered. By optimizing inventory levels, the retailer minimizes food waste while ensuring that fresh produce is always available to customers.

IMPLEMENTATION OF A SCENARIO

Scenario Overview:
A retail store sells various products, and it faces challenges with managing inventory:
- Stockouts lead to missed sales opportunities and dissatisfied customers.
- Overstocking results in higher holding costs and potential product obsolescence.

To optimize inventory levels, the retailer wants to predict future demand for each product using machine learning so they can stock the right number of products.

Objective:
We will use machine learning to predict demand for each product and, based on these predictions, suggest optimal reorder points and inventory levels.

Steps to Implement:
1. Generate synthetic sales data for multiple products.
2. Feature Engineering: Create features that include sales trends, seasonality, and product characteristics.
3. Model Training: Train a machine learning model (e.g., Random Forest) to predict future sales (demand) for each product.

4. Inventory Optimization: Based on predicted demand, calculate optimal reorder points and stock levels.

Let's implement this scenario:
Step-by-Step Code Implementation:

```python
# Import necessary libraries
import pandas as pd
import numpy as np
from sklearn.model_selection import train_test_split
from sklearn.ensemble import RandomForestRegressor
from sklearn.metrics import mean_absolute_error

# Parameters for synthetic data
num_products = 10
num_days = 365   # 1 year of sales data
product_ids = np.arange(1, num_products + 1)

df_sales =
pd.read_csv("D:/datasets/akularetailrevolution/inventory_
sales_data.csv")

# Step 2: Feature Engineering
# Add moving average and lagged features to capture sales
trends
df_sales['Lag_1'] =
df_sales.groupby('ProductID')['Sales'].shift(1).fillna(0)
df_sales['Lag_7'] =
df_sales.groupby('ProductID')['Sales'].shift(7).fillna(0)
# Last week's sales
df_sales['Rolling_Avg_7'] =
df_sales.groupby('ProductID')['Sales'].rolling(window=7).
mean().reset_index(0,

drop=True).fillna(0)

# Add day of the week as a feature (since sales may vary
by weekday)
df_sales['DayOfWeek'] = df_sales['Day'] % 7

# Drop rows with NaN values created by the lag features
df_sales = df_sales.dropna()
```

```python
# Step 3: Train-Test Split
X = df_sales.drop(columns=['Sales', 'ProductID'])  #
Features (excluding customer ID and sales)
y = df_sales['Sales']  # Target (sales)

# Split data into training and testing sets
X_train, X_test, y_train, y_test = train_test_split(X, y,
test_size=0.3, random_state=42)

# Step 4: Model Training - Random Forest Regressor for
sales prediction
rf_model = RandomForestRegressor(n_estimators=100,
random_state=42)
rf_model.fit(X_train, y_train)

# Predict sales on the test set
y_pred = rf_model.predict(X_test)

# Evaluate the model
mae = mean_absolute_error(y_test, y_pred)
print(f"Mean Absolute Error (MAE): {mae}")

# Step 5: Predict future sales for inventory optimization
# Simulate predicting sales for the next 30 days for each
product
future_days = 30
future_data = []
for product_id in product_ids:
    for day in range(num_days, num_days + future_days):
        # Get the last known sales for lag features
        last_day_sales = df_sales[df_sales['ProductID']
== product_id].iloc[-1]

        lag_1 = last_day_sales['Sales']
        lag_7 = df_sales[df_sales['ProductID'] ==
product_id].iloc[-7]['Sales'] if day > 6 else lag_1
        rolling_avg_7 = df_sales[df_sales['ProductID'] ==
product_id].iloc[-7:]['Sales'].mean()
        day_of_week = day % 7

        future_data.append([product_id, day, lag_1,
lag_7, rolling_avg_7, day_of_week])
```

```python
# Create a DataFrame for future predictions
df_future = pd.DataFrame(future_data,
columns=['ProductID', 'Day', 'Lag_1', 'Lag_7',
'Rolling_Avg_7', 'DayOfWeek'])

# Predict future sales for each product
df_future['Predicted_Sales'] =
rf_model.predict(df_future[['Day', 'Lag_1', 'Lag_7',
'Rolling_Avg_7', 'DayOfWeek']])

# Step 6: Inventory Optimization - Calculate Reorder
Points and Stock Levels
# Assuming the lead time for replenishment is 7 days and
a safety stock factor
lead_time = 7
safety_factor = 1.5   # 50% more stock for safety

# Calculate Reorder Point and Optimal Stock Level for
each product
inventory_plan = []
for product_id in product_ids:
    future_sales = df_future[df_future['ProductID'] ==
product_id]['Predicted_Sales']
    daily_demand = future_sales.mean()

    reorder_point = daily_demand * lead_time   # Expected
demand during lead time
    optimal_stock_level = reorder_point * safety_factor
# Adding safety stock

    inventory_plan.append([product_id, reorder_point,
optimal_stock_level])

# Create DataFrame for inventory plan
df_inventory_plan = pd.DataFrame(inventory_plan,
columns=['ProductID', 'ReorderPoint',
'OptimalStockLevel'])

# Display Inventory Plan
print("\nInventory Optimization Plan:\n",
df_inventory_plan)

# Step 7: Export the future predictions and inventory
```

```
plan to CSV files
df_future.to_csv("future_predictions.csv", index=False)
df_inventory_plan.to_csv("inventory_plan.csv",
index=False)

print("Future predictions and inventory plan have been
saved to CSV files.")
```

Output:
- Mean Absolute Error (MAE): A measure of the model's performance in predicting sales.
- Inventory Plan: A table with recommended reorder points and optimal stock levels for each product.

We can focus on other areas from where we left in the above code. Below is a continuation of the above discussion.

1. Sales Trends Analysis
- We can analyze predicted sales trends for each product over the next 30 days to identify products with high demand, declining trends, or potential stockouts.

```
# 1. Sales Trends Analysis
import matplotlib.pyplot as plt

# Step 1: Visualizing Predicted Sales Trends for the next
30 days
plt.figure(figsize=(12, 8))

for product_id in product_ids:
    product_data = df_future[df_future['ProductID'] ==
product_id]
    plt.plot(product_data['Day'] - num_days,
product_data['Predicted_Sales'], label=f'Product
{product_id}')

plt.title('Predicted Sales Trends for Next 30 Days')
plt.xlabel('Days into Future')
plt.ylabel('Predicted Sales')
plt.legend(title="Product ID")
plt.grid(True)
plt.show()
```

```
# Step 2: Identify Products with Highest and Lowest
Demand
# Calculate average predicted sales for each product over
the next 30 days
avg_predicted_sales =
df_future.groupby('ProductID')['Predicted_Sales'].mean().
reset_index()

# Sort to find highest and lowest demand products
highest_demand_product =
avg_predicted_sales.sort_values(by='Predicted_Sales',
ascending=False).iloc[0]
lowest_demand_product =
avg_predicted_sales.sort_values(by='Predicted_Sales',
ascending=True).iloc[0]

print(f"Product with highest demand: Product
{highest_demand_product['ProductID']}, Avg. Sales:
{highest_demand_product['Predicted_Sales']:.2f}")
print(f"Product with lowest demand: Product
{lowest_demand_product['ProductID']}, Avg. Sales:
{lowest_demand_product['Predicted_Sales']:.2f}")

# Step 3: Seasonal and Day-of-Week Analysis
# Analyze average predicted sales by day of the week
avg_sales_by_dayofweek =
df_future.groupby('DayOfWeek')['Predicted_Sales'].mean()

# Plot the average sales by day of the week
plt.figure(figsize=(8, 5))
avg_sales_by_dayofweek.plot(kind='bar', color='skyblue')
plt.title('Average Predicted Sales by Day of the Week')
plt.xlabel('Day of the Week (0 = Monday, 6 = Sunday)')
plt.ylabel('Average Predicted Sales')
plt.grid(True)
plt.show()
```

Explanation:

1. **Visualizing Predicted Sales Trends:**
   - We plot the predicted sales for each product over the next 30 days.
   - This helps visualize rising, falling, or fluctuating demand.

2. **Identifying Products with Highest and Lowest Demand:**
    o   We calculate the average predicted sales for each product.
    o   The product with the highest and lowest demand is identified based on the average sales over the 30 days.
3. **Seasonal and Day-of-Week Analysis:**
    o   We analyze how the day of the week impacts sales by calculating average predicted sales for each day of the week.

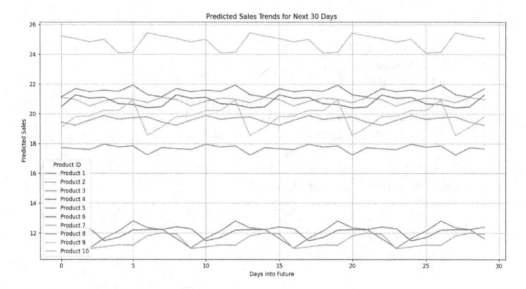

2. Inventory Cost Optimization

*   We can calculate the potential cost of holding too much inventory (overstock) or losing sales due to stockouts. This will help refine inventory management strategies.

```
# Define holding and stockout costs
holding_cost_rate_per_day = 0.02   # 2% of product value
per unit per day
stockout_cost_per_unit = 50   # Lost profit per unit in
case of stockout

# Assuming the product value for each product (in
monetary units)
product_values = np.random.randint(100, 500,
size=num_products)   # Random product values between 100
and 500

# Step 1: Calculate Holding Costs for Overstocking
```

```
inventory_costs = []
for product_id in product_ids:
    # Get the predicted daily demand for the next 30 days
    future_sales = df_future[df_future['ProductID'] ==
product_id]['Predicted_Sales'].mean()

    # Get reorder point and stock level from the previous
inventory plan
    reorder_point =
df_inventory_plan[df_inventory_plan['ProductID'] ==
product_id]['ReorderPoint'].values[0]
    optimal_stock_level =
df_inventory_plan[df_inventory_plan['ProductID'] ==
product_id]['OptimalStockLevel'].values[0]

    # Calculate holding costs
    overstock_units = max(optimal_stock_level -
future_sales, 0)
    holding_cost = overstock_units *
holding_cost_rate_per_day * product_values[product_id -
1] * future_days

    # Step 2: Calculate Stockout Costs
    stockout_units = max(future_sales -
optimal_stock_level, 0)
    stockout_cost = stockout_units *
stockout_cost_per_unit

    # Total cost
    total_cost = holding_cost + stockout_cost

    inventory_costs.append([product_id, holding_cost,
stockout_cost, total_cost])

# Create DataFrame for inventory cost analysis
df_inventory_cost = pd.DataFrame(inventory_costs,
columns=['ProductID', 'HoldingCost', 'StockoutCost',
'TotalCost'])

# Display the inventory cost analysis
print("\nInventory Cost Optimization Analysis:\n",
df_inventory_cost)
```

```
# Step 3: Identify the product with the highest total
cost
highest_cost_product =
df_inventory_cost.sort_values(by='TotalCost',
ascending=False).iloc[0]
print(
    f"\nProduct with the highest total cost: Product
{highest_cost_product['ProductID']}, Total Cost:
{highest_cost_product['TotalCost']:.2f}")

# Step 4: Plot total costs for each product
import matplotlib.pyplot as plt

plt.figure(figsize=(10, 6))
plt.bar(df_inventory_cost['ProductID'],
df_inventory_cost['TotalCost'], color='orange',
alpha=0.7)
plt.title('Total Inventory Costs for Each Product')
plt.xlabel('Product ID')
plt.ylabel('Total Cost (Holding + Stockout)')
plt.grid(True)
plt.show()
```

Explanation:

1. **Define Holding and Stockout Costs:**
   o **Holding costs:** 2% of the product value per unit per day (this can be adjusted based on real business data).
   o **Stockout costs:** Assumed as $50 per unit for lost sales (this can also be adjusted).

2. **Calculate Costs:**
   o **Holding costs** are calculated for overstocking (i.e., when the stock level exceeds demand).
   o **Stockout costs** are calculated when the predicted demand exceeds the available stock (leading to lost sales).

3. **Optimize Costs:**
   o We calculate the total cost for each product by summing holding and stockout costs.
   o The product with the highest total cost is identified, which could indicate where optimization is most needed.

4. **Visualize Costs:**
    - A bar plot is generated to compare all products' total inventory costs (holding + stockout).

3. Sensitivity Analysis

- Perform a sensitivity analysis to understand how changes in demand, lead time, or safety stock factor impact the reorder point and optimal stock levels.

```python
# Function to calculate inventory levels and costs based
on demand, lead time, and safety stock factor
def calculate_inventory_sensitivity(future_sales,
lead_time, safety_factor, product_value,
holding_cost_rate_per_day,

stockout_cost_per_unit):
    # Calculate reorder point and stock levels
    reorder_point = future_sales * lead_time
    optimal_stock_level = reorder_point * safety_factor

    # Calculate holding costs
    overstock_units = max(optimal_stock_level -
future_sales, 0)
    holding_cost = overstock_units *
holding_cost_rate_per_day * product_value * future_days

    # Calculate stockout costs
    stockout_units = max(future_sales -
optimal_stock_level, 0)
    stockout_cost = stockout_units *
stockout_cost_per_unit

    # Total cost
    total_cost = holding_cost + stockout_cost

    return reorder_point, optimal_stock_level, total_cost


# Define base parameters
holding_cost_rate_per_day = 0.02   # 2% of product value
per unit per day
stockout_cost_per_unit = 50   # Lost profit per unit in
```

```
case of stockout
lead_time = 7  # Base lead time
safety_factor = 1.5  # Base safety stock factor

# Step 1: Demand Sensitivity (10% increase and decrease
in demand)
sensitivity_analysis = []
for product_id in product_ids:
    # Get average future sales for the product
    future_sales = df_future[df_future['ProductID'] ==
product_id]['Predicted_Sales'].mean()
    product_value = product_values[product_id - 1]

    # Calculate base case
    base_reorder, base_stock, base_cost =
calculate_inventory_sensitivity(future_sales, lead_time,
safety_factor,
                    product_value,
holding_cost_rate_per_day, stockout_cost_per_unit)

    # Demand +10%
    increased_demand = future_sales * 1.10
    incr_reorder, incr_stock, incr_cost =
calculate_inventory_sensitivity(increased_demand,
lead_time, safety_factor,
                    product_value,
holding_cost_rate_per_day, stockout_cost_per_unit)

    # Demand -10%
    decreased_demand = future_sales * 0.90
    decr_reorder, decr_stock, decr_cost =
calculate_inventory_sensitivity(decreased_demand,
lead_time, safety_factor,
                    product_value, holding_cost_rate_per_day,
stockout_cost_per_unit)

    # Append results
    sensitivity_analysis.append(
        [product_id, base_reorder, incr_reorder,
decr_reorder, base_stock, incr_stock, decr_stock,
base_cost, incr_cost,
        decr_cost])
```

```
# Step 2: Lead Time Sensitivity (+20% and -20%)
for product_id in product_ids:
    # Get average future sales for the product
    future_sales = df_future[df_future['ProductID'] ==
product_id]['Predicted_Sales'].mean()
    product_value = product_values[product_id - 1]

    # Lead Time +20%
    increased_lead_time = lead_time * 1.20
    incr_lead_reorder, incr_lead_stock, incr_lead_cost =
calculate_inventory_sensitivity(future_sales,
            increased_lead_time,safety_factor,
product_value, holding_cost_rate_per_day,
stockout_cost_per_unit)

    # Lead Time -20%
    decreased_lead_time = lead_time * 0.80
    decr_lead_reorder, decr_lead_stock, decr_lead_cost =
calculate_inventory_sensitivity(future_sales,
        decreased_lead_time,safety_factor,
product_value,holding_cost_rate_per_day,stockout_cost_per
_unit)

    # Append results
    sensitivity_analysis.append(
        [product_id, incr_lead_reorder,
decr_lead_reorder, incr_lead_stock, decr_lead_stock,
incr_lead_cost,
        decr_lead_cost])

# Step 3: Safety Stock Sensitivity (adjusting safety
stock factor)
for product_id in product_ids:
    # Get average future sales for the product
    future_sales = df_future[df_future['ProductID'] ==
product_id]['Predicted_Sales'].mean()
    product_value = product_values[product_id - 1]

    # Safety Stock Factor +20%
    increased_safety_factor = safety_factor * 1.20
    incr_safety_reorder, incr_safety_stock,
incr_safety_cost =
calculate_inventory_sensitivity(future_sales, lead_time,
```

```
                    increased_safety_factor,
product_value,holding_cost_rate_per_day,stockout_cost_per
_unit)

    # Safety Stock Factor -20%
    decreased_safety_factor = safety_factor * 0.80
    decr_safety_reorder, decr_safety_stock,
decr_safety_cost =
calculate_inventory_sensitivity(future_sales, lead_time,
      decreased_safety_factor, product_value,
holding_cost_rate_per_day,stockout_cost_per_unit)

    # Append results
    sensitivity_analysis.append(
        [product_id, incr_safety_reorder,
decr_safety_reorder, incr_safety_stock,
decr_safety_stock, incr_safety_cost,
        decr_safety_cost])

# Convert results to a DataFrame for further analysis
columns = ['ProductID', 'BaseReorder',
'IncreasedReorder', 'DecreasedReorder', 'BaseStock',
'IncreasedStock',
            'DecreasedStock', 'BaseCost', 'IncreasedCost',
'DecreasedCost']
df_sensitivity_analysis =
pd.DataFrame(sensitivity_analysis, columns=columns)

# Display Sensitivity Analysis results
print("\nSensitivity Analysis:\n",
df_sensitivity_analysis)
```

Explanation:

1. **Demand Sensitivity**:
   o We evaluate how a 10% **increase** and 10% **decrease** in demand affect the reorder points, stock levels, and costs.
2. **Lead Time Sensitivity**:
   o We simulate a 20% **increase** and 20% **decrease** in lead time to see how inventory levels and costs are affected.
3. **Safety Stock Sensitivity**:

     ○   We adjust the **safety stock factor** by ±20% to see how it impacts the reorder point, stock levels, and overall inventory costs.

Expected Output:
- The analysis will display the results of how changing demand, lead time, and safety stock factor affects:
  - **Reorder Points**
  - **Optimal Stock Levels**
  - **Total Inventory Costs (holding + stockout)**

This will help identify which factors are the most sensitive and where the inventory strategy can be optimized for better performance and cost savings.

4. Stockout Probability Estimation
- Estimate the probability of stockouts based on demand fluctuations and inventory levels.

```python
# 4. Stockout Probability Estimation

from scipy.stats import norm


# Function to estimate stockout probability based on
predicted demand and stock levels
def calculate_stockout_probability(mean_demand,
std_demand, available_stock):
    # Probability of stockout is the probability that
demand exceeds stock
    stockout_prob = norm.sf(available_stock,
loc=mean_demand, scale=std_demand)
    return stockout_prob


# Define standard deviation for demand fluctuations
(assume 20% of mean demand for simplicity)
demand_variability_factor = 0.20

# Step 1: Estimate Stockout Probabilities for Each
Product
stockout_probabilities = []
for product_id in product_ids:
    # Get the mean predicted sales for the next 30 days
```

```
    future_sales = df_future[df_future['ProductID'] ==
product_id]['Predicted_Sales']
    mean_demand = future_sales.mean()
    std_demand = mean_demand * demand_variability_factor
# Assume 20% fluctuation in demand

    # Get reorder point and stock level from the
inventory plan
    available_stock =
df_inventory_plan[df_inventory_plan['ProductID'] ==
product_id]['OptimalStockLevel'].values[0]

    # Calculate stockout probability
    stockout_prob =
calculate_stockout_probability(mean_demand, std_demand,
available_stock)

    # Append results
    stockout_probabilities.append([product_id,
mean_demand, std_demand, available_stock, stockout_prob])

# Create DataFrame for stockout probabilities
df_stockout_prob = pd.DataFrame(stockout_probabilities,
                                columns=['ProductID',
'MeanDemand', 'StdDemand', 'AvailableStock',

'StockoutProbability'])

# Display Stockout Probability Analysis
print("\nStockout Probability Estimation:\n",
df_stockout_prob)

# Step 2: Identify products with the highest stockout
risk
high_risk_products =
df_stockout_prob[df_stockout_prob['StockoutProbability']
> 0.3]
print("\nProducts with high stockout risk (>30%
probability):\n", high_risk_products)

# Step 3: Plot stockout probabilities for each product
import matplotlib.pyplot as plt
```

```
plt.figure(figsize=(10, 6))
plt.bar(df_stockout_prob['ProductID'],
df_stockout_prob['StockoutProbability'], color='red',
alpha=0.7)
plt.title('Stockout Probability for Each Product')
plt.xlabel('Product ID')
plt.ylabel('Stockout Probability')
plt.grid(True)
plt.show()
```

Explanation:

1. **Demand Distribution**:
   - o We assume that demand follows a **normal distribution** with a mean equal to the predicted demand and a standard deviation equal to 20% of the mean demand (this variability can be adjusted based on business data).

2. **Stockout Probability Calculation**:
   - o For each product, the probability of a **stockout** is calculated using the **Survival Function (sf)** of the normal distribution, which gives the probability that demand exceeds the available stock (stockout event).

3. **High-Risk Products**:
   - o Products with a **stockout probability** higher than 30% are identified as **high-risk** products. These products may require immediate attention, such as increasing stock levels or adjusting reorder points.

4. **Visualizing Stockout Probability**:
   - o A **bar chart** is generated to visualize the stockout probability for each product, helping the retailer easily identify products with high stockout risks.

The **Stockout Probability Estimation** analysis shows that none of the products currently have a significant risk of stockouts. All products have a **stockout probability of 0%**, indicating that their available stock levels (Optimal Stock Levels) are sufficiently high to meet the predicted demand, even with demand fluctuations of 20%.

This suggests that the current inventory strategy effectively prevents stockouts, at least for the products analyzed in this scenario. However, we could refine the model further by adjusting the demand variability factor or exploring other risk scenarios.

The **bar chart** also visualizes the stockout probabilities for each product; as expected, the stockout probabilities are low.

CASE STUDIES ON SUCCESSFUL IMPLEMENTATION

CASE STUDY 1: WALMART

Walmart uses sophisticated machine learning algorithms to manage its inventory, particularly in optimizing stock levels and predicting seasonal fluctuations. This allows the retail giant to meet customer demand without overstocking, reducing both costs and waste.

CASE STUDY 2: ZARA

Zara's approach to inventory management is driven by its fast fashion model, where speed and responsiveness are key. Using advanced predictive models, Zara forecasts trends and customer preferences, allowing for rapidly restocking popular items and reducing underperforming stock.

CASE STUDY 3: AMAZON

Amazon employs complex algorithms to manage its massive inventory across global fulfillment centers. Machine learning aids in predicting buying trends, optimizing stock levels, and managing logistical operations, ensuring timely delivery and high customer satisfaction.

Conclusion

Integrating machine learning into inventory management transforms traditional practices into dynamic systems that significantly enhance operational efficiency and customer satisfaction. Predictive models and AI-driven tools enable businesses to forecast demand accurately, optimize logistics, and reduce wastage, ensuring that inventory levels align with market demand. As technology advances, adopting these tools is becoming advantageous and essential for retail businesses aiming to stay competitive in a rapidly changing market.

Retailers that leverage AI for inventory management will be able to respond to demand in real-time, reduce excess stock, prevent stockouts, and ultimately improve their financial health.

* * *

CHAPTER 5

PRICING OPTIMIZATION

In the fiercely competitive retail landscape, pricing strategy can be the difference between thriving and merely surviving. This chapter explores how artificial intelligence (AI) and machine learning (ML) are revolutionizing the way businesses approach pricing through dynamic pricing models. We delve into the strategies for competitive pricing that not only boost profits but also enhance customer satisfaction and market positioning.

The Role of AI in Pricing Optimization

AI in pricing optimization refers to the use of advanced algorithms and machine learning techniques to set prices dynamically based on various market factors and consumer behavior. This allows businesses to respond in real-time to changes in demand, competitor strategies, and other external factors.

UNDERSTANDING DYNAMIC PRICING MODELS POWERED BY AI

Fundamentals of Dynamic Pricing

Dynamic pricing, also known as surge pricing or demand pricing, involves adjusting prices on the fly in response to market demand and other variables. AI enhances this approach by analyzing large datasets to predict how these changes affect consumer buying decisions.

AI Techniques Used in Dynamic Pricing

1. **Predictive Analytics:** Utilizes historical data and algorithms to forecast consumer demand and price elasticity.

2. **Machine Learning Models:** Employs models like regression analysis, decision trees, and neural networks to continually learn from pricing outcomes and refine the pricing strategy.

3. **Real-Time Data Processing:** Integrates real-time analytics to adjust prices based on current market conditions.

Project: Dynamic Pricing Optimization for Retail Using Machine Learning

In a retail business, pricing products dynamically can significantly impact revenue and customer satisfaction. Dynamic pricing allows retailers to adjust prices based on real-time data such as demand, competitor prices, stock levels, and customer behavior. The goal of this project is to create a machine learning model that predicts the optimal price for each product based on historical sales data, stock levels, demand fluctuations, and competitor prices, maximizing the revenue and maintaining an optimal balance between inventory levels and customer satisfaction.

Key Objectives:
1. Predict optimal prices for products based on historical data.
2. Adjust prices dynamically to maximize revenue while ensuring customer satisfaction.
3. Ensure inventory levels are balanced to prevent overstocking or stockouts.

DATASET:

To create a dataset for this problem, the following features can be included:

1. **Product ID**: Unique identifier for each product.
2. **Date**: Date of the transaction or observation.
3. **Sales Volume**: Number of units sold on a particular day.
4. **Price**: The price at which the product was sold on a particular day.
5. **Competitor Price**: The average price of competitors for the same product on the given day.
6. **Stock Levels**: Number of units available in the inventory for a given day.
7. **Promotion/Discount**: Any promotions or discounts applied to the product on the given day.
8. **Demand Forecast**: Forecasted demand for the product on a given day.
9. **Seasonality**: Information about whether the product is seasonal (e.g., holidays, special events).
10. **Customer Ratings**: Average rating for the product based on customer feedback.

Product_ID	Date	Sales_Volume	Price	Competitor_Price	Stock_Levels	Promotion	Demand_Forecast	Seasonality	Customer_Ratings
101	2023-10-01	50	20.0	19.5	100	0	60	1	4.2
102	2023-10-01	40	15.0	14.8	80	1	50	0	4.0
103	2023-10-02	35	30.0	29.5	70	0	45	0	4.3
101	2023-10-02	60	19.0	19.0	90	1	65	1	4.5

Implementation:

Let's implement the Dynamic Pricing with simple implementation:

```python
# Import libraries
import pandas as pd
from sklearn.model_selection import train_test_split
from sklearn.ensemble import RandomForestRegressor
from sklearn.metrics import mean_squared_error
import matplotlib.pyplot as plt
```

Here, we are importing essential libraries:

- **Pandas**: Used for data manipulation and handling the dataset (DataFrames).
- **train_test_split** from sklearn.model_selection: Used to split the dataset into training and testing sets.
- **RandomForestRegressor** from sklearn.ensemble: This is the machine learning algorithm (Random Forest) that will be used to predict the optimal product price.
- **mean_squared_error** from sklearn.metrics: A metric used to evaluate the performance of the model. It measures the average squared difference between actual and predicted prices.
- **matplotlib.pyplot**: Used for data visualization, such as plotting the importance of features in the model.

```python
# Load dataset (Replace this with your dataset path or
data loading process)
data =
pd.read_csv("D:/datasets/akularetailrevolution/dynamic_pr
icing_dataset.csv")
```

Reading the dataset discussed earlier.

```
# Convert date to datetime and extract useful time-based
features
data['Date'] = pd.to_datetime(data['Date'])
data['Day'] = data['Date'].dt.day
data['Month'] = data['Date'].dt.month
data['Year'] = data['Date'].dt.year

# Drop the original date column and Product_ID (for
simplicity)
data = data.drop(columns=['Date', 'Product_ID'])
```

- **Date Conversion**: We convert the Date column from string format to datetime so we can extract meaningful time-based features, like the day, month, and year.
- **Feature Extraction**: From the Date column, we extract three features: Day, Month, and Year, which can provide more insight into pricing trends, seasonality, or demand fluctuations over time.
- **Dropping Columns**: We drop Date (since we already extracted relevant information) and Product_ID (for simplicity) from the feature set.

```
# Define features (X) and target (y)
X = data.drop(columns='Price')
y = data['Price']
```

Here, we define:
- **Features (X)**: These are the independent variables used to predict the price. They include:
  - Sales_Volume
  - Competitor_Price
  - Stock_Levels
  - Promotion
  - Demand_Forecast
  - Seasonality
  - Customer_Ratings
  - Day, Month, Year (time-based features extracted earlier)
- **Target (y)**: This is the dependent variable we want to predict—i.e., the **Price** of the product.

```
# Split the data into training and testing sets
X_train, X_test, y_train, y_test = train_test_split(X, y,
test_size=0.2, random_state=42)
```

We split the dataset into:

- **Training Set** (80%): Used to train the model.
- **Test Set** (20%): Used to evaluate the performance of the model after training.

The random_state=42 ensures that the splitting process is consistent each time the code is run.

```
# Create a RandomForestRegressor model
model = RandomForestRegressor(n_estimators=100,
random_state=42)

# Train the model
model.fit(X_train, y_train)
```

- **RandomForestRegressor**: We use the Random Forest algorithm, which is an ensemble method combining multiple decision trees to improve prediction accuracy and reduce overfitting. The number of trees (n_estimators) is set to 100.
- **Training the Model**: The model is trained using the training data (X_train, y_train).

```
# Make predictions
y_pred = model.predict(X_test)
```

After the model is trained, we use it to predict prices on the test set (X_test). The predictions are stored in y_pred.

```
# Evaluate the model
mse = mean_squared_error(y_test, y_pred)
rmse = mse ** 0.5

print(f"Root Mean Squared Error: {rmse}")
```

- **Mean Squared Error (MSE)**: This metric calculates the average squared difference between the actual and predicted prices. It helps to measure how well the model is performing.
- **Root Mean Squared Error (RMSE)**: The square root of the MSE gives us RMSE, which is easier to interpret because it is in the same units as the target variable (Price). A lower RMSE indicates better performance.

```
# Feature Importance
importances = model.feature_importances_
feature_names = X.columns
indices = importances.argsort()[::-1]

# Plot the feature importance
plt.figure(figsize=(10, 6))
plt.title("Feature Importance in Price Prediction")
plt.barh(range(len(indices)), importances[indices],
align='center')
plt.yticks(range(len(indices)), [feature_names[i] for i
in indices])
plt.xlabel("Relative Importance")
plt.show()
```

- **Feature Importance**: Random Forest models can provide insights into which features are most important in making predictions. The feature_importances_ attribute of the trained model gives a numerical value indicating the importance of each feature.
- **Plotting Feature Importance**: The code plots the importance of each feature, allowing you to visualize which factors (such as Demand_Forecast, Stock_Levels, or Competitor_Price) have the greatest influence on price prediction.

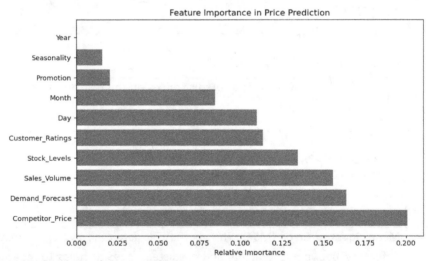

Root Mean Squared Error: 12.095

This basic implementation can be enhanced further by experimenting with hyperparameters, trying different machine-learning algorithms, or incorporating additional business-specific features into the dataset.

STRATEGIES FOR COMPETITIVE PRICING AND MAXIMIZING PROFITS

Competitor Price Tracking

AI systems can monitor competitor pricing in real time, providing insights that help businesses adjust their prices competitively. Tools like web scrapers and API integrations collect pricing data across different platforms, ensuring that a business's pricing strategy remains competitive.

Price Elasticity Modeling

Understanding price elasticity — how the quantity demanded of a product change in response to price changes — is crucial for effective dynamic pricing. AI models analyze past pricing changes and their impact on sales to determine the optimal price points for various products.

Price Elasticity of Demand (PED) measures how sensitive the quantity demanded of a product is to changes in its price. The formula for price elasticity is:

$$\text{Price Elasticity of Demand (PED)} = \frac{\%\text{ change in quantity demanded}}{\%\text{ change in price}}$$

If the elasticity is:
- **Elastic**: PED < -1 (Demand is very responsive to price changes).
- **Inelastic**: -1 < PED < 0 (Demand is less responsive to price changes).
- **Unit Elastic**: PED = -1 (Proportional change in demand and price).

We can implement a simple price elasticity model using Python. The model will take historical sales and pricing data and calculate the elasticity.

Implementation:
- Calculate percentage changes in price and sales.
- Calculate price elasticity using the formula.
- Analyze whether demand is elastic or inelastic based on the computed value.

```
import pandas as pd
import numpy as np

# Generate a simple dataset for demonstration
data = pd.DataFrame({
    'Date': pd.date_range(start='2023-01-01', periods=10,
freq='D'),
```

```
    'Price': [10, 11, 12, 13, 12, 11, 10, 9, 8, 7],   #
Simulating price changes
    'Sales_Volume': [100, 95, 85, 80, 90, 95, 110, 120,
130, 140]   # Sales affected by price changes
})

# Calculate percentage change in Price and Sales Volume
data['Price_Change_%'] = data['Price'].pct_change() * 100
data['Sales_Change_%'] =
data['Sales_Volume'].pct_change() * 100

# Calculate Price Elasticity of Demand
data['Price_Elasticity'] = data['Sales_Change_%'] /
data['Price_Change_%']

# Display the dataset with Price Elasticity values
print(data)

# Analyze the Price Elasticity
def elasticity_analysis(row):
    if row['Price_Elasticity'] < -1:
        return 'Elastic'
    elif -1 <= row['Price_Elasticity'] < 0:
        return 'Inelastic'
    else:
        return 'Undefined'

# Apply the analysis
data['Elasticity_Type'] = data.apply(elasticity_analysis,
axis=1)

# Show final data
print(data[['Date', 'Price', 'Sales_Volume',
'Price_Elasticity', 'Elasticity_Type']])
```

Explanation:
1. **Dataset:**
    o   We create a simple dataset that includes a series of prices and corresponding sales volumes over 10 days.
    o   The Price column represents the price changes of a product.
    o   The Sales_Volume column represents the sales volume, which may change in response to price changes.

2. **Percentage Change**:
   - o Price_Change_%: This column calculates the percentage change in price from one day to the next.
   - o Sales_Change_%: This column calculates the percentage change in sales volume from one day to the next.
3. **Price Elasticity Calculation**:
   - o The formula for **Price Elasticity** is applied: Sales_Change_% / Price_Change_%.
4. **Elasticity Analysis**:
   - o Based on the price elasticity values, we categorize whether the demand is **Elastic, Inelastic**, or **Undefined** (if the result is NaN or the price hasn't changed).
5. **Output**:
   - o The final output includes the date, price, sales volume, calculated price elasticity, and the type of elasticity (elastic/inelastic).

The code will generate output like this:

```
         Date  Price  Sales_Volume  Price_Elasticity Elasticity_Type
0  2023-01-01     10           100               NaN       Undefined
1  2023-01-02     11            95         -0.500000       Inelastic
2  2023-01-03     12            85         -1.157895         Elastic
3  2023-01-04     13            80         -0.705882       Inelastic
4  2023-01-05     12            90         -1.625000         Elastic
5  2023-01-06     11            95         -0.666667       Inelastic
6  2023-01-07     10           110         -1.736842         Elastic
7  2023-01-08      9           120         -0.909091       Inelastic
8  2023-01-09      8           130         -0.750000       Inelastic
9  2023-01-10      7           140         -0.615385       Inelastic
```

Analysis:

1. **Inelastic Demand**: When Price_Elasticity is between -1 and 0, the demand is less sensitive to price changes. The changes in sales volume are smaller relative to price changes.
2. **Elastic Demand**: When Price_Elasticity is less than -1, demand is elastic, meaning the sales volume is more responsive to price changes.
3. **Undefined**: In cases where price doesn't change or there is missing data, elasticity is undefined.

Retailers can use price elasticity models to:
- **Understand Customer Sensitivity**: Discover how sensitive customers are to price changes for different products.

- **Optimize Pricing Strategies**: By knowing which products have elastic or inelastic demand, retailers can strategically adjust prices to maximize revenue.
- **Discount Optimization**: For products with inelastic demand, even small price increases may lead to increased revenue without much loss in demand, whereas for elastic products, discounts may drive significant sales.

This is a simplified example and can be extended with more sophisticated methods such as using machine learning models to predict demand based on price elasticity trends across larger datasets.

Segmentation and Personalization

AI enables price optimization at the customer segment level, allowing for personalized pricing strategies. AI can identify which segments are more price-sensitive by analyzing customer data and adjust prices accordingly to maximize sales volume and profit margins.

Example: Segment customers based on their purchase behavior
Note: This implementation is done using synthetic data generated.

In this implementation, we will segment customers based on their purchase behavior using **K-Means Clustering**, and then create a personalized recommendation for each customer segment. The model will analyze customer data and group them into distinct segments based on features like purchasing frequency, average order value, and discount sensitivity. After segmentation, we will personalize recommendations or pricing strategies for each segment.

Problem Statement: The goal is to use AI to segment customers based on their purchasing behavior and personalize pricing strategies or product recommendations accordingly. Segments will be identified using features such as purchase frequency, average order value, and discount sensitivity.

Features:

- **Customer_ID**: Unique identifier for each customer.
- **Purchase Frequency**: Number of purchases made by the customer in a given period (e.g., per month).
- **Average Order Value (AOV)**: The average amount the customer spends per purchase.
- **Discount Sensitivity**: A binary indicator of whether the customer tends to buy more often when discounts are applied.

- **Engagement Level**: A score representing how engaged the customer is (e.g., through website visits, email opens, etc.).

Steps:

1. **Data Generation**: Create a synthetic dataset to represent customer purchase behavior.

2. **Customer Segmentation**: Use K-Means Clustering to group customers based on similar behaviors.

3. **Personalization**: Provide different pricing or product recommendations based on the identified segments.

```python
import pandas as pd
import numpy as np
from sklearn.cluster import KMeans
import matplotlib.pyplot as plt
from sklearn.preprocessing import StandardScaler

# Step 1: Create a synthetic dataset representing
customer behavior
np.random.seed(42)
num_customers = 100   # Number of customers

data = pd.DataFrame({
    'Customer_ID': range(1, num_customers + 1),
    'Purchase_Frequency': np.random.randint(1, 10,
num_customers),   # Purchases per month
    'Avg_Order_Value': np.random.uniform(50, 500,
num_customers),   # Average amount spent per purchase
    'Discount_Sensitivity': np.random.choice([0, 1],
num_customers),   # Tendency to buy with discounts (0 =
no, 1 = yes)
    'Engagement_Level': np.random.uniform(0, 100,
num_customers)   # Engagement score (e.g., website visits,
email opens)
})

# Step 2: Standardize the data (to ensure features are on
the same scale)
scaler = StandardScaler()
data_scaled =
scaler.fit_transform(data[['Purchase_Frequency',
'Avg_Order_Value', 'Discount_Sensitivity',
'Engagement_Level']])
```

```python
# Step 3: Use K-Means Clustering to segment customers
kmeans = KMeans(n_clusters=3, random_state=42)  # Set
number of clusters (segments) to 3
data['Segment'] = kmeans.fit_predict(data_scaled)

# Step 4: Analyze the customer segments
segment_summary = data.groupby('Segment').mean()
print("Segment Summary:")
print(segment_summary)

# Step 5: Visualize the clusters (for demonstration,
using 2 features)
plt.figure(figsize=(8, 6))
plt.scatter(data['Purchase_Frequency'],
data['Avg_Order_Value'], c=data['Segment'],
cmap='viridis')
plt.xlabel('Purchase Frequency')
plt.ylabel('Avg Order Value')
plt.title('Customer Segmentation Based on Purchase
Behavior')
plt.colorbar(label='Segment')
plt.show()

# Step 6: Define personalized recommendations based on
segments
def personalize_recommendations(row):
    if row['Segment'] == 0:
        return 'Offer Premium Products'
    elif row['Segment'] == 1:
        return 'Provide Discounts and Offers'
    elif row['Segment'] == 2:
        return 'Increase Engagement with Loyalty
Programs'

# Apply personalized recommendations to each segment
data['Personalized_Recommendation'] =
data.apply(personalize_recommendations, axis=1)

# Step 7: Show the final dataset with segments and
personalized recommendations
print(data[['Customer_ID', 'Segment',
'Personalized_Recommendation']].head(10))
```

```
# Optional: Save the dataset to a CSV file
data.to_csv('customer_segmentation_and_personalization.cs
v', index=False)
```

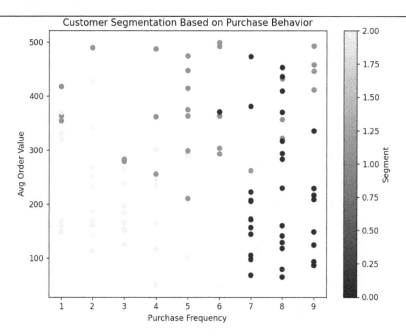

Sample Output:

```
   Customer_ID  Segment              Personalized_Recommendation
0            1        0                      Offer Premium Products
1            2        1                   Provide Discounts and Offers
2            3        1                   Provide Discounts and Offers
3            4        1                   Provide Discounts and Offers
4            5        0                      Offer Premium Products
5            6        2  Increase Engagement with Loyalty Programs
6            7        0                      Offer Premium Products
7            8        0                      Offer Premium Products
8            9        2  Increase Engagement with Loyalty Programs
9           10        2  Increase Engagement with Loyalty Programs
```

We calculate the average feature values for each segment to understand the characteristics of each group. For example, one segment may have high engagement and purchase frequency, while another may be highly discount-sensitive.

Visualization:

To visualize the clusters, we create a scatter plot using two features, Purchase_Frequency and Avg_Order_Value. Customers are colored based on their assigned segment. This gives a visual representation of how the algorithm grouped customers.

Personalized Recommendations:

For each segment, we provide personalized pricing or product recommendations:

- **Segment 0**: Customers with high average order values may receive offers for premium products.
- **Segment 1**: Customers who are price-sensitive may be offered discounts or promotional offers.
- **Segment 2**: Customers with lower engagement may be targeted with loyalty programs to increase retention.

Final Dataset:

The final dataset includes:

- **Customer_ID**: The unique identifier for each customer.
- **Segment**: The segment (cluster) the customer belongs to.
- **Personalized_Recommendation**: The tailored recommendation or pricing strategy for each customer based on their segment.

Integration with Promotional Strategies

AI not only optimizes base pricing but also aligns with promotional strategies. By analyzing the effectiveness of past promotions, AI can predict the optimal timing and depth of discounts for future campaigns, maximizing the impact on sales and profits.

Example: The model will identify which customer segments are more price-sensitive and will allow for targeted pricing to maximize both sales and profits.

Note: This implementation is done using synthetic data generated.

Steps:

1. **Data Preparation**: We'll create synthetic data that represents customer behavior, including features like customer purchase frequency, average order value, and engagement metrics.
2. **Customer Segmentation**: Using **K-Means Clustering**, we'll segment customers into groups based on these features.
3. **Price Sensitivity Analysis**: After segmentation, we'll label the segments based on their price sensitivity, allowing for personalized pricing strategies.

Features:

- **Customer_ID**: Unique identifier for each customer.
- **Purchase Frequency**: The average number of purchases per month.

- **Average Order Value**: The average amount spent per purchase.
- **Discount Sensitivity**: A binary indicator of whether the customer tends to purchase more when discounts are applied.
- **Engagement Level**: A score representing how engaged the customer is (e.g., visits the website, opens emails).
- **Price Sensitivity**: A target variable we will calculate later based on clustering.

```python
import pandas as pd
import numpy as np
from sklearn.cluster import KMeans
import matplotlib.pyplot as plt
from sklearn.preprocessing import StandardScaler

# Step 1: Create a synthetic dataset representing
customer behavior
np.random.seed(42)
num_customers = 200

data = pd.DataFrame({
    'Customer_ID': range(1, num_customers + 1),
    'Purchase_Frequency': np.random.randint(1, 10,
num_customers),  # Purchases per month
    'Avg_Order_Value': np.random.uniform(50, 500,
num_customers),  # Average amount spent per purchase
    'Discount_Sensitivity': np.random.choice([0, 1],
num_customers),  # Tendency to buy with discounts
    'Engagement_Level': np.random.uniform(0, 100,
num_customers)  # Engagement score (e.g., website visits,
email opens)
})

# Step 2: Standardize the data (to ensure features are on
the same scale)
scaler = StandardScaler()
data_scaled =
scaler.fit_transform(data[['Purchase_Frequency',
'Avg_Order_Value', 'Discount_Sensitivity',
'Engagement_Level']])

# Step 3: Use K-Means Clustering to segment customers
kmeans = KMeans(n_clusters=3, random_state=42)
```

```
data['Segment'] = kmeans.fit_predict(data_scaled)

# Step 4: Analyze the customer segments
# Calculate the mean of each feature in each cluster to
interpret them
segment_summary = data.groupby('Segment').mean()

print("Segment Summary:")
print(segment_summary)

# Step 5: Visualize the clusters (for demonstration,
using 2 features)
plt.figure(figsize=(8, 6))
plt.scatter(data['Purchase_Frequency'],
data['Avg_Order_Value'], c=data['Segment'],
cmap='viridis')
plt.xlabel('Purchase Frequency')
plt.ylabel('Avg Order Value')
plt.title('Customer Segmentation Based on Purchase
Behavior')
plt.colorbar(label='Segment')
plt.show()

# Step 6: Add labels for price sensitivity based on
cluster characteristics
# For simplicity, we'll assume customers in the highest
Purchase Frequency and Discount Sensitivity segments are
price sensitive

def label_price_sensitivity(row):
    if row['Segment'] ==
segment_summary['Purchase_Frequency'].idxmax() or
row['Segment'] ==
segment_summary['Discount_Sensitivity'].idxmax():
        return 'Price Sensitive'
    else:
        return 'Not Price Sensitive'

data['Price_Sensitivity'] =
data.apply(label_price_sensitivity, axis=1)

# Step 7: Show the final dataset with Segmentation and
Price Sensitivity
```

```
print(data[['Customer_ID', 'Segment',
'Price_Sensitivity']].head(10))

# Optional: Save the dataset to a CSV file
data.to_csv('customer_segmentation_and_pricing.csv',
index=False)
```

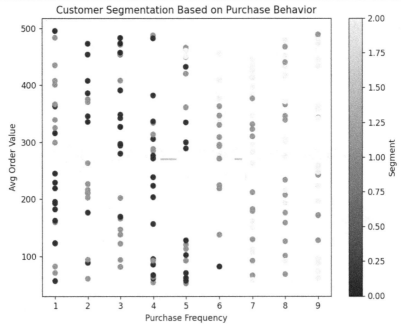

Explanation:

1. **Data Generation:**

   o We generate a synthetic dataset with 200 customers, where each customer has features like Purchase_Frequency, Avg_Order_Value, Discount_Sensitivity, and Engagement_Level.

   o These features represent customer behavior in terms of how often they purchase, how much they typically spend, how sensitive they are to discounts, and their overall engagement.

2. **Feature Scaling:**

   o Before applying machine learning algorithms, we use StandardScaler to standardize the features. This ensures that all features have a mean of 0 and a standard deviation of 1, which helps with clustering algorithms like K-Means.

3. **K-Means Clustering:**

○ We use **K-Means Clustering** to segment the customers into 3 clusters. The algorithm divides customers into groups based on their similarities in purchasing behavior, discount sensitivity, and engagement.

○ The result is a new column, Segment, that indicates which group a customer belongs to.

4. **Segment Summary**:

○ We calculate the average values of the features for each segment. This helps us interpret the segments and understand their characteristics (e.g., which segment buys frequently, which is more discount-sensitive, etc.).

5. **Visualization**:

○ A scatter plot is created to visualize the clusters based on Purchase_Frequency and Avg_Order_Value. The different colors represent different segments.

6. **Price Sensitivity Labeling**:

○ We create a simple rule-based system to label customers as either "Price Sensitive" or "Not Price Sensitive."

○ For this, we assume that the segment with the highest purchase frequency or the highest discount sensitivity is price-sensitive.

7. **Output**:

○ The final dataset includes the customer segment and their associated price sensitivity label.

○ The output can be saved as a CSV file for further use.

Sample Output:

```
     Customer_ID  Segment    Price_Sensitivity
0              1        2        Price Sensitive
1              2        0    Not Price Sensitive
2              3        1        Price Sensitive
3              4        1        Price Sensitive
4              5        2        Price Sensitive
```

CHALLENGES AND ETHICAL CONSIDERATIONS

While dynamic pricing offers numerous advantages, it also presents significant challenges and ethical concerns. These issues need careful consideration to ensure that the approach benefits both the business and the customer without compromising trust, fairness, or legal integrity. Below are the major challenges and ethical considerations:

1. Customer Perception and Trust:

Challenge:

- Frequent and unpredictable price changes can cause frustration and erode customer trust. If customers perceive pricing to be arbitrary or unfair, they may feel manipulated or exploited, leading to a loss of loyalty.

- Transparency is key when implementing dynamic pricing. However, explaining why prices fluctuate based on demand, time, or customer behavior can be difficult, especially when customers don't fully understand the reasons behind it.

Ethical Consideration:

- **Fairness**: Customers must believe that pricing is fair and equitable. If two customers see dramatically different prices for the same product, particularly in the absence of clear justification, it can be perceived as unfair.

- **Communication**: Businesses must ensure that they communicate price changes effectively, emphasizing the factors that influence pricing. For instance, airlines often explain that prices increase as fewer seats are available to manage expectations.

- **Avoiding Discrimination**: Dynamic pricing models that use personal data for price adjustments, such as geographical location, purchasing history, or browsing patterns, must avoid discriminatory practices. For example, charging different prices based on income levels or ZIP codes can lead to ethical dilemmas and even legal consequences.

Mitigation:

- Transparent pricing policies and clear communication regarding the factors influencing price changes can mitigate these concerns.

- Offering customers the ability to understand and anticipate price changes (e.g., through notifications of upcoming discounts) can help maintain trust.

2. Regulatory Compliance:

Challenge:

- Implementing dynamic pricing requires businesses to comply with a variety of laws and regulations, especially when using customer data to inform pricing strategies. Regulations may vary across regions and industries, making compliance complex.

- In industries like airlines, ride-sharing, and hotels, where dynamic pricing is common, there are often strict legal frameworks governing pricing practices. Failing to comply with these regulations can lead to fines, lawsuits, or other legal consequences.

Ethical Consideration:

- **Price Gouging**: During emergencies or crises (e.g., natural disasters, pandemics), dynamic pricing models can inadvertently result in price gouging—where prices skyrocket due to sudden spikes in demand. While higher prices may reflect true supply constraints, they can also exploit vulnerable customers in urgent need.

- **Data Privacy and Security**: Dynamic pricing often relies on customer data to adjust prices. This raises privacy concerns, especially in regions with strict data protection laws like GDPR in Europe or CCPA in California. Businesses must ensure that they are using customer data responsibly and transparently.

- **Anti-competitive Practices**: In some cases, dynamic pricing may be viewed as anti-competitive or predatory, especially if it involves collusion or attempts to manipulate market conditions to the detriment of competitors or consumers.

Mitigation:

- Implementing strict internal compliance policies and working closely with legal experts to ensure that all pricing practices adhere to the relevant laws and guidelines in different jurisdictions.

- During crises, businesses should implement safeguards that prevent unethical price gouging by setting upper limits on price increases.

3. Algorithmic Bias and Unintended Discrimination:

Challenge:

- Dynamic pricing algorithms, especially those driven by AI and machine learning, may unintentionally introduce biases into pricing strategies. For example, certain customer groups may be unfairly charged higher prices if the model associates them with lower price sensitivity, even if this is based on biased or incomplete data.

Ethical Consideration:

- **Bias in Data**: If the training data used to develop pricing algorithms contains historical biases (e.g., geographic or demographic), it could lead to price discrimination. For example, customers from affluent areas may consistently be shown higher prices because the model has learned that they are more likely to make purchases regardless of price.

- **Discrimination**: AI-driven dynamic pricing could reinforce systemic inequalities if certain socioeconomic groups are disproportionately affected by higher prices. This is especially concerning in industries that provide essential goods and services, such as healthcare, utilities, and food.

Mitigation:

- Regular auditing and testing of dynamic pricing algorithms to identify and mitigate any potential biases.

- Ensuring diversity in the data used to train pricing models to reduce the risk of bias and unintended discrimination.

- Implementing guidelines that prevent the use of sensitive personal characteristics (e.g., race, gender, income level) directly or indirectly in pricing decisions.

4. Consumer Backlash and Negative Publicity:

Challenge:

- Companies that are seen as manipulating prices to maximize profit at the expense of customers may face public backlash. This is particularly true in cases where dynamic pricing is applied to essential products or during times of crisis.

- Consumer sentiment can shift quickly if people feel they are being taken advantage of, leading to negative reviews, media coverage, and social media backlash that can harm a company's reputation.

Ethical Consideration:

- **Public Sentiment**: Even when legally compliant, dynamic pricing strategies must consider public sentiment. Charging significantly higher prices during peak demand periods, such as holidays, can be perceived as exploitative and result in brand damage.

Mitigation:

- Balancing profit maximization with customer satisfaction by setting limits on how much prices can fluctuate, especially for regular customers.

- Offering loyalty programs or dynamic discount strategies for frequent customers to offset the perception of unfair price hikes.

5. Technological Reliability and Transparency:

Challenge:

- Dynamic pricing relies heavily on algorithms that must process large amounts of data in real-time. If the system fails—either due to poor design, inadequate testing, or unforeseen market conditions—prices may be set incorrectly, leading to revenue losses or customer dissatisfaction.

Ethical Consideration:

- **Algorithm Transparency**: Customers often have limited visibility into how dynamic pricing algorithms work, which can cause discomfort and lead to trust issues. Many customers are unaware of the factors that influence price changes, and opaque pricing models may exacerbate this concern.

Mitigation:

- Ensuring that dynamic pricing models are rigorously tested for accuracy and reliability before deployment, and continuously monitored to handle market anomalies or unexpected behavior.

- Providing transparency by offering clear, accessible explanations to customers about how prices are set, without disclosing proprietary algorithms.

6. Impact on Low-Income Customers:

Challenge:

- Dynamic pricing may inadvertently penalize low-income customers. If algorithms determine that these customers are less likely to purchase unless prices are lower, businesses might offer them discounted prices.

While this might seem beneficial in the short term, it can also reinforce negative stereotypes or limit access to premium products or services.

Ethical Consideration:

- **Exacerbating Inequality**: If dynamic pricing leads to consistently lower prices for certain demographics, it may limit their access to quality goods or create a two-tiered system where higher-paying customers receive better products or services.

Mitigation:

- Ensuring that dynamic pricing does not reinforce economic disparities, and considering social responsibility when designing pricing models.

- Offering equitable access to premium products and services, regardless of the customer's ability to pay more, and balancing profit motives with fairness.

CASE STUDIES ON SUCCESSFUL IMPLEMENTATION

CASE STUDY 1: UBER

Uber's use of dynamic pricing, particularly surge pricing during high demand periods, demonstrates the power of AI in optimizing prices in real-time based on immediate market conditions. This strategy not only balances supply and demand but also maximizes profits per ride.

CASE STUDY 2: AMAZON

Amazon's pricing strategy involves changing prices daily based on demand, competition, and inventory levels. Machine learning algorithms help predict the optimal prices for maximizing sales and profits, maintaining Amazon's competitive edge in the market.

CASE STUDY 3: AIRLINES INDUSTRY

Airlines have long used dynamic pricing models to adjust ticket prices based on various factors, including booking time, demand, season, and competitor pricing. AI has refined these models, allowing for more granular pricing decisions that maximize revenue per flight.

Conclusion

AI-driven dynamic pricing models represent a significant advancement in retail and service industries, providing businesses the tools to optimize their pricing strategies in real time. By embracing AI, companies can remain competitive in fluctuating markets and increase profitability and customer satisfaction. As AI technology evolves, its integration into pricing strategies will become increasingly sophisticated, offering even more excellent opportunities for businesses to thrive in competitive environments.

While dynamic pricing can significantly enhance profitability and operational efficiency, businesses must be aware of the associated challenges and ethical considerations. Transparency, fairness, and compliance with legal standards are essential to maintaining customer trust and avoiding negative consequences such as public backlash, regulatory penalties, or unintended bias. By addressing these challenges proactively, businesses can implement dynamic pricing strategies that are both effective and ethically sound.

* * *

CHAPTER 6

STORE LAYOUT OPTIMIZATION

The physical layout of a store plays a crucial role in influencing customer behavior, enhancing shopping experiences, and ultimately driving sales. This chapter explores how advancements in machine learning and data analytics are revolutionizing store layout optimization by leveraging customer footfall data and visual merchandising techniques. We will delve into strategies that enable retailers to create environments that not only appeal to consumer preferences but also maximize operational efficiency.

The Significance of Store Layout Optimization
A well-optimized store layout ensures that customers find what they are looking for while being introduced to other items that may catch their interest. Effective store layouts can lead to increased dwell times, higher conversion rates, and enhanced customer satisfaction. With the integration of AI and machine learning, retailers can now achieve a deeper understanding of how different layouts affect consumer behavior and sales performance.

ANALYZING CUSTOMER FOOTFALL DATA TO OPTIMIZE STORE LAYOUTS

Understanding Footfall Data

Footfall data refers to the information collected on the number of people entering a store, their movements within it, and the time they spend in various sections. This data is invaluable in understanding how customers interact with the store environment.

Technologies for Collecting Footfall Data
1. **Video Analytics:** CCTV and advanced video analytics provide insights into customer traffic patterns and dwell times.
2. **Wi-Fi Tracking:** Tracks devices that search for Wi-Fi networks, helping map customer routes through the store.

3. **Infrared Sensors:** Count customer entries and exits, offering data on peak times and store capacity usage.

Machine Learning Models for Footfall Analysis

- **Heat Maps Generation:** Machine learning algorithms analyze video and sensor data to create heat maps of customer activity, highlighting high-traffic areas and potential bottlenecks.

- **Customer Journey Mapping:** Advanced models can track the paths customers typically take, identifying strategic points for product placement and promotional displays.

Introduction to Footfall Analysis Using Machine Learning in Retail

In today's competitive retail environment, understanding customer footfall patterns is crucial for optimizing operations, managing resources effectively, and driving revenue growth. Footfall analysis allows businesses to predict the number of customers visiting a store based on a variety of factors, including time of day, weather conditions, holidays, and ongoing promotions. By leveraging the power of machine learning, retailers can forecast customer footfall and make data-driven decisions about staffing, inventory management, and marketing strategies.

This program provides a practical example of how to use machine learning, specifically the **Random Forest Regressor** model, to perform footfall prediction in retail. We simulate a dataset with relevant factors such as **day of the week**, **time of day**, **weather conditions**, **promotions**, and whether it's a holiday or weekend, and use these features to predict customer footfall.

Key benefits of footfall analysis using machine learning include:

- **Accurate staffing**: Predict footfall to avoid overstaffing or understaffing.

- **Optimized inventory**: Forecast customer flow to ensure sufficient stock is available during peak times.

- **Targeted promotions**: Align marketing campaigns with predicted footfall to maximize impact.

The program walks through data preparation, feature engineering, model training, evaluation, and visualization of the results. This is a practical starting point for retail managers and data analysts looking to harness AI for operational efficiency and enhanced decision-making.

Data Generation: We simulate retail footfall data using numpy. The features include:

- **DayOfWeek**: Which day of the week it is (1 = Monday, 7 = Sunday).
- **TimeOfDay**: Hour of the day.
- **IsHoliday**: Whether the day is a holiday or not.
- **WeatherCondition**: The weather condition on that day (0 = Clear, 1 = Rainy, 2 = Snowy).
- **Promotion**: Whether there's an ongoing promotion or not.
- **Footfall**: The actual number of visitors (target variable).

Program follows:

```python
import numpy as np
import pandas as pd
from sklearn.model_selection import train_test_split
from sklearn.ensemble import RandomForestRegressor
from sklearn.metrics import mean_absolute_error, r2_score
import matplotlib.pyplot as plt

# Step 1: Generate Sample Data for Footfall Analysis
np.random.seed(42)

# Generate 1000 samples of retail footfall data
data_size = 1000

data = {
    'DayOfWeek': np.random.randint(1, 8, size=data_size),
# 1 = Monday, 7 = Sunday
    'TimeOfDay': np.random.randint(0, 24,
size=data_size),   # Hours of the day
    'IsHoliday': np.random.randint(0, 2, size=data_size),
# 1 = Holiday, 0 = Non-holiday
    'WeatherCondition': np.random.randint(0, 3,
size=data_size),   # 0 = Clear, 1 = Rainy, 2 = Snowy
    'Promotion': np.random.randint(0, 2, size=data_size),
# 1 = Promotion, 0 = No promotion
    'Footfall': np.random.randint(50, 500,
size=data_size)   # Actual footfall (target variable)
}

# Convert the data into a pandas DataFrame
```

```
df = pd.DataFrame(data)

# Step 2: Feature Engineering - Create "Weekend" Feature
df['IsWeekend'] = df['DayOfWeek'].apply(lambda x: 1 if x
>= 6 else 0)

# Step 3: Split the dataset into features (X) and target
(y)
X = df[['DayOfWeek', 'TimeOfDay', 'IsHoliday',
'WeatherCondition', 'Promotion', 'IsWeekend']]
y = df['Footfall']

# Step 4: Split data into training and testing sets
X_train, X_test, y_train, y_test = train_test_split(X, y,
test_size=0.3, random_state=42)

# Step 5: Train the RandomForestRegressor Model
model = RandomForestRegressor(n_estimators=100,
random_state=42)
model.fit(X_train, y_train)

# Step 6: Make Predictions
y_pred = model.predict(X_test)

# Step 7: Evaluate the Model
mae = mean_absolute_error(y_test, y_pred)
r2 = r2_score(y_test, y_pred)

print(f"Mean Absolute Error (MAE): {mae}")
print(f"R-squared (R2): {r2}")

# Step 8: Visualize the Actual vs Predicted Footfall
plt.figure(figsize=(10,6))
plt.scatter(range(len(y_test)), y_test, color='blue',
label='Actual Footfall', alpha=0.6)
plt.scatter(range(len(y_pred)), y_pred, color='red',
label='Predicted Footfall', alpha=0.6)
plt.title('Actual vs Predicted Footfall')
plt.xlabel('Samples')
plt.ylabel('Footfall')
plt.legend()
plt.show()
```

This program is focused on **predicting retail footfall** using a **Random Forest Regressor** model. Footfall analysis helps retail businesses understand customer behavior and forecast the number of people visiting their stores based on various factors such as day of the week, time of day, weather, and promotions.

Here's a breakdown of the key steps in the code:

Imports:

- **numpy (np)**: Used for numerical operations and generating random data.
- **pandas (pd)**: Used to manage and manipulate the dataset, creating data frames from the generated data.
- **train_test_split**: A utility from sklearn.model_selection to split the dataset into training and testing sets.
- **RandomForestRegressor**: A machine learning model used for regression tasks, part of the sklearn.ensemble library.
- **mean_absolute_error, r2_score**: Metrics to evaluate the performance of the model.
- **matplotlib.pyplot (plt)**: Used for plotting graphs to visualize results.

Step 1: Generate Sample Data for Footfall Analysis

- **np.random.seed(42)**: Ensures that the random data generated is reproducible.
- The program generates a dataset of **1000 samples** for different features:
    - **DayOfWeek**: A random integer between 1 (Monday) and 7 (Sunday).
    - **TimeOfDay**: A random integer between 0 and 23, representing the hour of the day.
    - **IsHoliday**: A binary feature (0 = Non-holiday, 1 = Holiday).
    - **WeatherCondition**: Random weather conditions (0 = Clear, 1 = Rainy, 2 = Snowy).
    - **Promotion**: Whether there's an ongoing promotion (0 = No, 1 = Yes).
    - **Footfall**: The actual number of people visiting the store, generated randomly between 50 and 500.
- These variables will serve as **features** (independent variables) and the **footfall** as the target (dependent variable) for the prediction model.

Step 2: Feature Engineering - Creating "Weekend" Feature

- A new feature IsWeekend is derived from the **DayOfWeek**. It flags whether a day is a weekend (Saturday or Sunday, i.e., if DayOfWeek >= 6).

Step 3: Split the Data into Features (X) and Target (y)

- **X**: Independent variables or features used to predict the target variable:

    o DayOfWeek, TimeOfDay, IsHoliday, WeatherCondition, Promotion, IsWeekend.

- **y**: The target variable (Footfall), which represents the actual footfall we want to predict.

Step 4: Train-Test Split

- The dataset is split into **training** and **testing** sets using train_test_split(). 70% of the data is used for training (X_train, y_train), and 30% for testing (X_test, y_test). This allows us to evaluate how well the model generalizes to unseen data.

Step 5: Train the Random Forest Regressor Model

- The **RandomForestRegressor** model is trained using the training data (X_train, y_train).

- **n_estimators=100**: The number of decision trees in the forest.

- **random_state=42**: Ensures reproducibility of results.

Random Forest is an ensemble method that builds multiple decision trees and averages their predictions to improve accuracy and reduce overfitting.

Step 6: Make Predictions

- The trained model predicts the footfall on the testing data (X_test) using model.predict(), and stores the predictions in y_pred.

Step 7: Model Evaluation

- **Mean Absolute Error (MAE)**: Measures the average magnitude of the errors between the predicted and actual values. Lower MAE indicates better accuracy.

- **R-squared (R^2)**: Measures how well the model fits the data. It ranges from 0 to 1, where a higher value indicates that the model explains a larger portion of the variance in the target variable.

Output:

Mean Absolute Error (MAE): 123.44515781746033
R-squared (R2): -0.1780801645711061

Step 8: Visualizing the Actual vs Predicted Footfall

- A **scatter plot** is used to compare the actual and predicted footfall.
    - **Blue points** represent the actual footfall.
    - **Red points** represent the predicted footfall.
- This visualization helps to visually inspect how closely the predicted values match the actual footfall data.

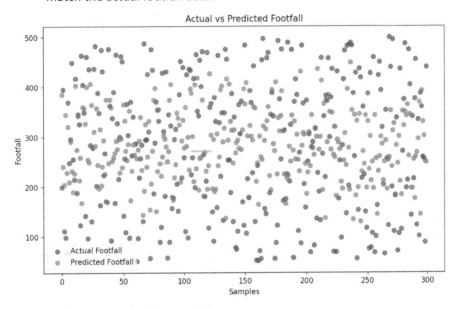

You can further customize the model by:

- Using real-world footfall data from retail stores.
- Incorporating additional features such as **events, temperature, competitor promotions**, or **store location**.
- Experimenting with other models such as **Gradient Boosting, XGBoost**, or **Neural Networks** for better accuracy.

This machine learning model could help retail managers optimize store operations, forecast staffing needs, and strategize marketing campaigns based on expected footfall.

MACHINE LEARNING APPLICATIONS IN VISUAL MERCHANDISING

Enhancing Product Placement with AI

Machine learning algorithms can analyze sales data alongside footfall patterns to determine the optimal placement of products. For example, high-margin products can be positioned in high-traffic areas to increase visibility and impulse purchases.

Personalized Display Recommendations

AI can tailor store displays to match the preferences of the local customer base, changing layouts based on demographic insights derived from loyalty program data and purchase history.

Dynamic Merchandising

Using real-time data, stores can dynamically adjust their layouts and displays to adapt to changing consumer trends, seasonal demands, or promotional strategies. Machine learning models facilitate rapid response to these variables, ensuring the store environment remains optimized for current market conditions.

Implementing Layout Changes

Pilot Testing: Before a full-scale rollout, AI-driven layout recommendations should be pilot tested in selected stores to measure their impact on sales and customer experience. This testing allows for adjustments based on real-world feedback.

Integration with Store Operations: Optimal layouts need to consider not just customer experience but also store operations. Machine learning can help balance customer flow with restocking efficiency and checkout placement to minimize operational disruptions.

Training and Change Management: Store staff should be trained on the reasons behind layout changes and how to leverage them to improve sales and customer interaction. Effective change management practices are essential to ensure smooth transitions and staff buy-in.

Machine Learning Implementation

To implement **Machine Learning applications in Visual Merchandising**, we can create a program that predicts the impact of various visual merchandising factors (like window display design, shelf arrangement, product placement, lighting, etc.) on store performance metrics such as sales or footfall. For this example, we will focus on predicting **sales performance** based on several visual merchandising attributes.

Steps to Implement:

1. **Dataset**: A dataset containing different visual merchandising attributes (window display, shelf arrangement, product placement) and the corresponding sales figures.
2. **Goal**: Train a model to predict the impact of these merchandising factors on sales.
3. **Model**: We'll use **Random Forest Regressor** to predict sales performance.

Example Dataset (You can modify this or load your own):

Let's assume we have a dataset with the following columns:

- **WindowDisplayQuality**: Rating of window display (1 to 5)

- **ShelfArrangementQuality**: Rating of shelf arrangement (1 to 5)

- **ProductPlacementQuality**: Rating of product placement (1 to 5)

- **LightingQuality**: Rating of lighting quality in the store (1 to 5)

- **Footfall**: Number of visitors to the store.

- **PromotionActive**: Whether a promotion is active (0 = No, 1 = Yes)

- **Sales**: Actual sales revenue (target variable)

```python
# Step 1: Import necessary libraries
import numpy as np
import pandas as pd
from sklearn.model_selection import train_test_split
from sklearn.ensemble import RandomForestRegressor
from sklearn.metrics import mean_absolute_error,
r2_score
import matplotlib.pyplot as plt

# Step 2: Create a sample dataset for visual
merchandising and sales performance
data = {
    'WindowDisplayQuality': np.random.randint(1, 6,
size=500),  # Ratings from 1 to 5
    'ShelfArrangementQuality': np.random.randint(1, 6,
size=500),  # Ratings from 1 to 5
    'ProductPlacementQuality': np.random.randint(1, 6,
size=500),  # Ratings from 1 to 5
    'LightingQuality': np.random.randint(1, 6,
size=500),  # Ratings from 1 to 5
    'Footfall': np.random.randint(50, 500, size=500),
# Number of visitors
    'PromotionActive': np.random.randint(0, 2,
size=500),  # 0 = No, 1 = Yes
    'Sales': np.random.randint(1000, 10000, size=500)
# Sales revenue (target variable)
}
```

```python
# Step 3: Convert the data into a pandas DataFrame
df = pd.DataFrame(data)

# Step 4: Split the dataset into features (X) and
target variable (y)
X = df[['WindowDisplayQuality',
'ShelfArrangementQuality', 'ProductPlacementQuality',
'LightingQuality', 'Footfall', 'PromotionActive']]
y = df['Sales']

# Step 5: Split the dataset into training and testing
sets (70% training, 30% testing)
X_train, X_test, y_train, y_test = train_test_split(X,
y, test_size=0.3, random_state=42)

# Step 6: Train the Random Forest Regressor model
model = RandomForestRegressor(n_estimators=100,
random_state=42)
model.fit(X_train, y_train)

# Step 7: Make predictions using the test set
y_pred = model.predict(X_test)

# Step 8: Evaluate the model performance using Mean
Absolute Error and R-squared
mae = mean_absolute_error(y_test, y_pred)
r2 = r2_score(y_test, y_pred)

print(f"Mean Absolute Error (MAE): {mae}")
print(f"R-squared (R2): {r2}")

# Step 9: Visualize the Actual vs Predicted Sales
plt.figure(figsize=(10,6))
plt.scatter(range(len(y_test)), y_test, color='blue',
label='Actual Sales', alpha=0.6)
plt.scatter(range(len(y_pred)), y_pred, color='red',
label='Predicted Sales', alpha=0.6)
plt.title('Actual vs Predicted Sales Performance')
plt.xlabel('Samples')
plt.ylabel('Sales')
plt.legend()
```

```
plt.show()

# Step 10: Feature Importance
feature_importance = model.feature_importances_
feature_names = X.columns

plt.figure(figsize=(10,6))
plt.barh(feature_names, feature_importance)
plt.title('Feature Importance in Predicting Sales')
plt.xlabel('Importance')
plt.ylabel('Features')
plt.show()
```

Explanation:

1. **Dataset Creation**:

   o We simulate a dataset containing ratings for different visual merchandising aspects (like **Window Display Quality**, **Shelf Arrangement Quality**, etc.) along with store **Footfall**, and whether there's an ongoing **Promotion**.

   o **Sales** is the target variable we aim to predict.

2. **Feature Engineering**:

   o We split the dataset into **X** (the features) and **y** (the target variable, i.e., Sales).

   o We include features such as window display ratings, footfall, promotion activity, etc.

3. **Model**:

   o We use the **RandomForestRegressor** to model and predict sales based on these visual merchandising factors.

4. **Model Evaluation**:

   o We evaluate the model's performance using **Mean Absolute Error (MAE)** and **R-squared (R^2)**. A lower MAE and higher R^2 value indicate better performance.

5. **Visualization**:

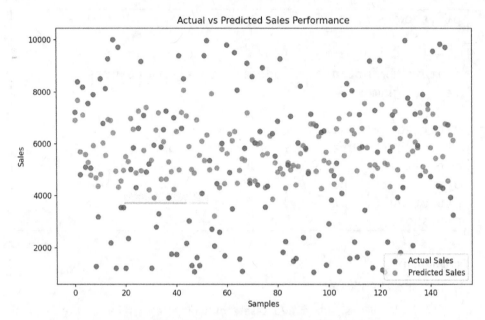

Figure 2: Actual v Predicted Sales (Visual Merchandising)

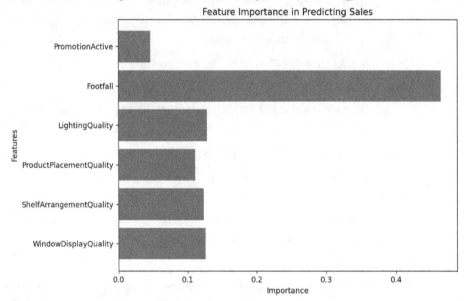

Figure 3: Feature importance for visual merchandising

o We plot the **Actual vs Predicted Sales** to visually see how well the model is predicting.

o We also plot **Feature Importance** to understand which merchandising factors (window display, shelf arrangement, etc.) have the most impact on sales performance.

Customization and Further Improvements:

- You can replace this simulated dataset with **real-world data** from your retail store.

- Add more features such as **seasonal factors**, **store size**, **store location**, or other **marketing efforts**.

- You can experiment with other machine learning models like **Gradient Boosting**, **XGBoost**, or **Neural Networks** to improve the accuracy of the predictions.

This type of machine learning application can help retailers **optimize their visual merchandising strategies** by understanding how each element affects store performance, allowing them to adjust displays, promotions, and product placements to maximize sales.

CASE STUDIES ON SUCCESSFUL STORE LAYOUT OPTIMIZATION

CASE STUDY 1: WALMART - LEVERAGING DATA ANALYTICS FOR STORE LAYOUT OPTIMIZATION

Walmart, one of the world's largest retailers, has integrated data analytics extensively into its operations, particularly in optimizing **store layouts**. By gathering and analyzing vast amounts of **customer footfall** and **purchase data**, Walmart identifies high-traffic areas within its stores and which sections attract the most customers. This analysis provides insights into customer behavior, such as popular shopping routes, dwell times in specific sections, and the frequency of product purchases.

Walmart uses this information to strategically place **high-demand products** in areas with maximum visibility and foot traffic, encouraging impulse buys and cross-selling opportunitles. For example, essential everyday items may be placed near the back of the store, requiring customers to walk past other product categories. In addition, by identifying which complementary products are often bought together, Walmart arranges items in proximity to one another to encourage **bundling** and **add-on purchases**.

The result is a more efficient layout that enhances customer convenience while also driving **increased revenue**. This use of data analytics ensures that Walmart remains responsive to consumer needs while maximizing product visibility and cross-selling, ultimately optimizing the **in-store shopping experience**.

CASE STUDY 2: IKEA - USING MACHINE LEARNING TO ENHANCE STORE DESIGN

IKEA, the global home furnishings giant, is known for its unique store design, where customers follow a **fixed path** through the store, exposing them to a wide range of products. This **maze-like layout** is strategically designed to maximize **footfall across all sections**, increasing the likelihood of impulse buys and inspiring customers with home design ideas. Every visit to IKEA involves walking through a carefully designed route that showcases various product categories, from furniture to home accessories.

To further refine this design, IKEA leverages **machine learning** to analyze **customer flow data**. Using data from in-store sensors, cameras, and customer feedback, machine learning algorithms can identify bottlenecks, underutilized areas, or sections where customers spend more time. These insights allow IKEA to make **small but impactful adjustments** to the layout, such as reorganizing displays, widening aisles, or adjusting the flow of customers through certain areas.

By constantly refining the shopping path, IKEA not only improves the **customer shopping experience** but also enhances **basket sizes** by encouraging customers to explore more sections of the store. The seamless integration of machine learning with its already successful store layout strategy helps IKEA increase customer satisfaction and drive more **profitable transactions**.

CASE STUDY 3: NORDSTROM - AI-POWERED STORE LAYOUT OPTIMIZATION

Nordstrom, a leading fashion retailer, has embraced **artificial intelligence (AI)** to create personalized, optimized shopping environments for its customers. Nordstrom collects data from various channels, including **in-store sensors**, **online shopping behaviors**, and **social media interactions**. This multi-channel approach gives Nordstrom a deep understanding of customer preferences and trends.

By integrating AI with this rich dataset, Nordstrom is able to **analyze foot traffic**, **customer preferences**, and **purchase behavior** across different store locations and time periods. The AI models use this data to optimize **store layouts**, helping Nordstrom determine where to place high-demand items, how to arrange departments, and even where to locate fitting rooms for maximum convenience.

Nordstrom's use of AI goes beyond general layout optimization. The retailer uses AI to create **personalized shopping experiences** by tailoring product placements and promotions based on customer preferences. For example, if in-store sensors detect a customer spending significant time in the women's shoe section, AI might recommend expanding the shoe selection in that store location or offering personalized promotions.

This **holistic, data-driven approach** helps Nordstrom create shopping environments that feel customized to individual customers, making the in-store experience more **engaging and effective**. As a result, Nordstrom has been able to increase **customer satisfaction**, improve **sales performance**, and strengthen its **omni-channel presence** by aligning in-store layouts with digital shopping habits.

CONCLUSION

Store layout optimization using **machine learning** gives retailers a powerful tool to gain a **significant competitive advantage** in today's fast-evolving market. By leveraging AI and data-driven insights, retail spaces can be designed not only for **aesthetic appeal** but also to align with **consumer behavior** and **business objectives**, maximizing both the customer experience and operational efficiency. Machine learning enables retailers to analyze vast amounts of data, including customer footfall, shopping patterns, product preferences, and environmental factors, to make intelligent decisions on how to arrange products and design store layouts.

As technology advances, particularly in areas like **real-time data processing**, **predictive analytics**, and **sensor technology**, the ability to analyze and interpret **complex datasets** will improve even further. This will allow retailers to respond dynamically to customer preferences, optimize layouts more precisely, and **personalize shopping experiences** at an unprecedented level. The result will be greater **efficiency in inventory management**, **increased sales**, and enhanced **customer satisfaction**.

Moreover, these advancements will lead to the development of **smart retail spaces** that can adapt automatically based on real-time customer data, optimizing product placement, traffic flow, and promotional strategies on the go. In the future, **machine learning-driven layout optimization** will not only enhance **sales performance** but also reduce **operational costs** by ensuring that every square foot of the store is utilized to its fullest potential. Ultimately, retailers who adopt machine learning for store layout optimization will be better positioned to thrive in a highly competitive landscape, delivering **tailored experiences** that resonate with modern consumers and drive long-term business success.

* * *